The Hebrew Bible as Literature:
A Very Short Introduction

VERY SHORT INTRODUCTIONS are for anyone wanting a stimulating and accessible way into a new subject. They are written by experts and have been translated into more than 40 different languages.

The series began in 1995 and now covers a wide variety of topics in every discipline. The VSI library now contains more than 400 volumes—a Very Short Introduction to everything from Indian philosophy to psychology and American history—and continues to grow in every subject area.

Very Short Introductions available now:

ACCOUNTING Christopher Nobes
ADOLESCENCE Peter K. Smith
ADVERTISING Winston Fletcher
AFRICAN AMERICAN
    RELIGION Eddie S. Glaude Jr
AFRICAN HISTORY John Parker and
    Richard Rathbone
AFRICAN RELIGIONS
    Jacob K. Olupona
AGNOSTICISM Robin Le Poidevin
AGRICULTURE Paul Brassley and
    Richard Soffe
ALEXANDER THE GREAT
    Hugh Bowden
ALGEBRA Peter M. Higgins
AMERICAN HISTORY Paul S. Boyer
AMERICAN IMMIGRATION
    David A. Gerber
AMERICAN LEGAL HISTORY
    G. Edward White
AMERICAN POLITICAL
    HISTORY Donald Critchlow
AMERICAN POLITICAL PARTIES
    AND ELECTIONS L. Sandy Maisel
AMERICAN POLITICS
    Richard M. Valelly
THE AMERICAN PRESIDENCY
    Charles O. Jones
THE AMERICAN
    REVOLUTION Robert J. Allison
AMERICAN SLAVERY
    Heather Andrea Williams
THE AMERICAN WEST
    Stephen Aron

AMERICAN WOMEN'S HISTORY
    Susan Ware
ANAESTHESIA Aidan O'Donnell
ANARCHISM Colin Ward
ANCIENT ASSYRIA Karen Radner
ANCIENT EGYPT Ian Shaw
ANCIENT EGYPTIAN ART AND
    ARCHITECTURE Christina Riggs
ANCIENT GREECE Paul Cartledge
THE ANCIENT NEAR EAST
    Amanda H. Podany
ANCIENT PHILOSOPHY Julia Annas
ANCIENT WARFARE
    Harry Sidebottom
ANGELS David Albert Jones
ANGLICANISM Mark Chapman
THE ANGLO - SAXON AGE John Blair
THE ANIMAL KINGDOM
    Peter Holland
ANIMAL RIGHTS David DeGrazia
THE ANTARCTIC Klaus Dodds
ANTISEMITISM Steven Beller
ANXIETY Daniel Freeman and
    Jason Freeman
THE APOCRYPHAL GOSPELS
    Paul Foster
ARCHAEOLOGY Paul Bahn
ARCHITECTURE Andrew Ballantyne
ARISTOCRACY William Doyle
ARISTOTLE Jonathan Barnes
ART HISTORY Dana Arnold
ART THEORY Cynthia Freeland
ASTROBIOLOGY David C. Catling
ASTROPHYSICS James Binney

Available soon:

For more information visit our web site

www.oup.com/vsi/

Tod Linafelt

THE HEBREW BIBLE AS LITERATURE

A Very Short Introduction

OXFORD
UNIVERSITY PRESS

OXFORD
UNIVERSITY PRESS

Oxford University Press is a department of the University of Oxford.
It furthers the University's objective of excellence in research, scholarship,
and education by publishing worldwide. Oxford is a registered trade mark of
Oxford University Press in the UK and certain other countries.

Published in the United States of America by Oxford University Press
198 Madison Avenue, New York, NY 10016, United States of America

© Oxford University Press 2016

Library of Congress Cataloging-in-Publication Data
Names: Linafelt, Tod, 1965– author.
Title: The Hebrew Bible as literature: a very short introduction
/Tod Linafelt.
Description: New York: Oxford University Press, [2016] | 2016 |
Series: Very short introductions | Includes index.
Identifiers: LCCN 2015037845| ISBN 9780195300079 (paperback)
| ISBN 9780199910472 (ebook) | ISBN 9780190262662 (ebook)
Subjects: LCSH: Bible. Old Testament—Introductions. | Bible. Old
Testament—Criticism, interpretation, etc. | Bible—Canon.
Classification: LCC BS1140.3 .L56 2016 | DDC 809/.935221—dc23
LC record available at http://lccn.loc.gov/2015037845

1 3 5 7 9 8 6 4 2

Printed in Great Britain
by Ashford Colour Press Ltd., Gosport, Hants.
on acid-free paper

Contents

Introduction

It has become increasingly clear in recent years that the Hebrew Bible (or the Christian Old Testament) contains some of the finest literature that we have, and biblical literature has begun to take its place not only in the synagogue and the church but also among the classics of world literature. Yet its place on that shelf cannot simply be presumed; it must be demonstrated by reference to and analysis of the literature itself. It is not enough to just assert the literary value of the Bible, as if such value were a given, nor is it the case that all of biblical literature is equally compelling or shows equal evidence of literary artfulness. But the Hebrew Bible has quite a few literary high points, and by focusing on those high points we can reclaim the achievements of ancient Israelite writers for world literature.

The stories of Jacob and David, for example, present what are probably the earliest surviving examples of literary characters whose development the reader follows over the length of a lifetime, watching as they are shaped by forces both internal and external, by factors and events that range from the personal to the familial to the political to, of course, the theological. These are characters who, unusual for ancient literature, carry the weight of their own pasts and who are consequently different in middle age than they were in their youths, and different still when we see them, in their old age, striving to hold on to a hard-won authority that slowly has begun to slip away from them.

Elsewhere, in shorter narratives such as the book of Ruth or the book of Esther, one finds more of a snapshot, in which a character is presented to the reader at some particular, fraught moment that will define his or her character, which, though lacking the depth of a narrated past, is nonetheless complex and ambiguous. Moreover, with Ruth and Esther we get the added complication of female heroines in a world of male power.

In addition to such prose narrative texts, the Hebrew Bible contains a substantial body of carefully wrought poetry. Most familiar, no doubt, is the book of Psalms, which has functioned not only as prayer book for the church and synagogue but also as a sourcebook for poets, establishing an emotional register that ranges from the elevations of unfettered praise ("You have turned my mourning into dancing!") to the emotional abyss of lament ("My God, my God, why have you forsaken me?"). The psalms are an important precedent for what is sometimes called "the lyric I," the unnamed first-person voice that we hear in so much early modern and contemporary poetry, from Shakespeare's "Shall I compare thee to a summer day?" to Paul Laurence Dunbar's poem "Sympathy" (with its final line "I know why the caged bird sings!").

Less well known, perhaps, is that the Bible also contains an especially fine sequence of erotic poetry in the Song of Songs (also known as the Song of Solomon), which makes effective use of metaphor, double entendre, and shifts in voice and tone in order to convey the pleasures (and to a lesser degree the threats) of young love. And in both the Psalms and the Song of Songs, as well as in other poems inset within narratives, we see poets at work as they manipulate structure, balance rhythms, and repeat keywords.

In short, the Bible can be read not only as *religious* literature, which is how most people think of it, but quite simply *as literature*.

Religion, history, literature

For centuries the Bible was read primarily as a religious document. Although its historical veracity went largely unquestioned and its literary power implicitly evident in the ways it influenced both prose and poetry in the West, it is nevertheless the case that for close to two millennia the Bible was read neither as history nor as literature but rather as a source for theological and ethical teachings. In other words, one went to the Bible to learn about God or to learn about how to live one's life in an appropriately pious way, rather than to experience or reflect upon its aesthetic qualities. It is true that the classical literary critic Longinus (or "Pseudo-Longinus"), writing in the first century CE, makes a brief reference to the opening lines of Genesis in his treatise *On the Sublime*, but the context for the reference is his treatment of "greatness of thought" rather than any strictly literary qualities. More typical of premodern literary attitudes toward the Bible is Augustine's judgment that biblical literature exhibits "the lowest of linguistic style" (*humillimum genus loquendi*) and had seemed to him, before his conversion, "unworthy of comparison with the majesty of Cicero." There are, to be sure, exceptions, with particular interpreters, both Jewish and Christian, exhibiting an especially keen literary sensibility, but such a sensibility was almost without fail put in the service of religiously oriented interpretation.

With the rise and spread of modern biblical criticism in the eighteenth and nineteenth centuries, the academic study of the Bible, if not the popular study, became overwhelmingly concerned with the historical value of the Bible. This historical orientation took one of two forms. First, there was, and remains, an interest in reconstructing the events presented in the Bible. For example, early modern academic critics would expend much energy in trying to demonstrate whether Noah's flood, recounted in Genesis 6–9, actually took place. Recent scholars would be more apt to argue over whether the story of David represents real political

3

history. Second, a historical approach might be less concerned with proving or disproving events recounted in the Bible and more with dating the biblical texts themselves. By placing the biblical stories, poems, and laws in a social, cultural, and historical context, modern scholarship helps explain what gave rise to these texts and what purposes they might have originally served.

But only in the last few decades of the twentieth century did there arise a genuine, sustained appreciation of the Bible's literary art, regardless of its historical veracity or its religious value. This is not to say that one cannot be interested in all three realms—religion, history, and literature—and of course there will be times when they overlap. In reading the Bible as literature, then, one may make use of historical data or contribute to historical analysis, just as one may engage religious or theological questions. But we now have a well-defined discipline of literary criticism of the Bible, and we can now talk with more confidence about the sometimes distinctive art of biblical literature.

What does it mean to read the Bible "as literature"?

Literature itself is notoriously hard to define. Indeed, some philosophers and literary theorists have challenged the very existence of something that we might refer to as "literature," arguing that what counts as literature is always culturally and socially defined, and that therefore there is nothing intrinsically "literary" to be identified. Such a position finds support in the fact that just about any strategy or technique—such as metaphor, heightened diction, suspenseful plotting, etc.—that one finds being used in "literature" can be found in other contexts, including not only polished writing such as formal speeches and essays but also in informal letters and even in e-mails or text messages. One way of responding to this observation might be to argue that a certain layered density of such literary strategies pushes a given piece of writing into the realm of literature; or that a speaker or author might strive for a "literary" effect without actually producing "literature." Winston Churchill's prose writings, Abraham Lincoln's speeches, the sermons of Martin Luther King Jr., the journals of Sylvia Plath, and many contemporary popular song lyrics—all of these are examples of richly literary works that may or may not count as literature, depending on one's perspective.

I will not presume to solve the ongoing debate about the nature and limits of literature. It is a debate both important and interesting and one that gives every sign of being essentially unsolvable. Rather, I will focus on the two traditional literary genres that we find in the Bible, namely narrative and poetry. (Drama, a third primary genre of literature, is not represented in the Bible.) Narrative trades in stories, with characters and events presented by a narrator, usually in the form of a plot with conflict or tension that builds and is resolved. Narrative can take the form of either prose (e.g., *Anna Karenina*, *The Great Gatsby*, and the Harry Potter novels) or poetry (e.g., the *Iliad*, *Beowulf*, and *Paradise Lost*); though as it happens, biblical narrative is always prose. Poetry in the Bible, on the other hand, is always essentially nonnarrative and tends to fall into the category of "lyric": short poems, generally spoken in the first person, which tend to focus on the inner life of the speaker as opposed to presenting a plot with characters and action. (Classical examples of lyric poetry include the work of the ancient Greek poets Sappho and Pindar, and the ancient Roman poets Horace and Catullus; modern examples would include the poems of Emily Dickinson, Dylan Thomas, Robert Frost, Langston Hughes, Marianne Moore, and virtually every poem published in *Poetry* magazine or the *New Yorker*.)

That the present book largely forgoes the complicated debate over defining literature is indicative of the fact that it contains a minimum of what is known as "literary theory," which is not quite the same thing as "literary criticism." Literary theory tends to reflect on the nature and boundaries of literature and its place in society, and it draws quite a bit on philosophy and social theory for its methods; literary criticism tends to jump right in to what is already defined as literature and thus identify the strategies and conventions for how that literature works. The former tends to be, as the phrase suggests, more "theoretical," the latter more "practical." While some scholars who are engaged in literary criticism or poetics dislike and dismiss theoretical concerns, I do not. I think that literary theory is vital to the study of literature and can be fascinating, and it has made great inroads into biblical studies. This Very Short Introduction, however, is more practical than theoretical, aiming to give readers the tools for recognizing and interpreting the literary workings of the Bible, largely by modeling such interpretation on selected texts. As a note to the reader, the biblical quotes in this book tend to follow the New Revised Standard Version (NRSV) translation, but I have sometimes modified them with reference to the Hebrew.

Literature as "a made thing"

Although we now use the word poetry to distinguish verse from prose, it used to have a much broader meaning and could refer to any literary work. Our term "poetry" goes back to the ancient Greek *poiein*, meaning "to make" or "to create." Literature, on this account, is "a made thing," which we might usefully understand in two ways. The first understanding lies behind the clichéd phrase "creative writing" or as it is sometimes called "imaginative literature," and emphasizes the essentially fictive nature of literature: it creates a textual world that is not strictly moored to the empirical world of everyday life. The second understanding focuses on literature as something made in the sense of something crafted, something highly constructed, the product of deliberate and sustained fashioning. Our word for fiction reveals a similar etymology, coming as it does from the Latin *facio* ("to do" or "to make") and its cognate *fictio* ("to fashion" or "to form"). Further reinforcing the roots of this understanding of literature as a crafted, made thing is the fact that the word "text" comes from the Latin *textus*, meaning something woven, fabricated ("fabric"), or built. Naturally, not all literary works will exhibit the same level of craft, but we can approach these works with an eye toward the layered constructedness that constitutes the woven texture of the text.

What might it mean to read the Bible as literature, as "a made thing" in both senses of that phrase? It means, in the first instance, to be willing to find in biblical literature an imaginatively created world—or better, a *linguistically* created world—and to allow for the possibility of being absorbed into that world as we read. With such imaginative, linguistic creations the question is not so much "Am I persuaded?" as one might ask in the case of more straightforwardly theological or philosophical literature, but rather "Am I transported?" How does or how might the literature of the Bible, especially in the case of narrative, take one out of the everyday into another, fictive world or, in the case of poetry, give one language that resonates with experience as if the words came from within rather than without? But we want as well to go beyond experiencing the Bible as literature to analyzing it, and so in the second instance to read it as literature means to read closely and analytically, with an eye toward details and technique. To do justice to literary works is to pay good, skillful attention not only to *what* is said but to *how* it is said. Rather than being content with a knowledge of the paraphrasable content of the biblical material, we will want to explore how it is that the literature achieves what it achieves.

Reflecting on the nature of literature, the Russian American novelist and critic Vladimir Nabokov has written:

> Literature was not born the day when a boy crying "wolf, wolf" came running out of the Neanderthal valley with a big gray wolf at his heels: literature was born on the day when a boy came crying "wolf, wolf" and there was no wolf behind him.

It is a quote worth pondering in several respects, but one point especially is appropriate to end these introductory reflections: namely, that literature is not primarily about communicating information. The boy crying "wolf, wolf" when there is no wolf behind him is not alerting others to the presence of danger, but is instead exploiting the human ability to use language in ways that go beyond communication—whether to startle and provoke, as our "wolf"-crying boy seems to intend, or to soothe and comfort, as may be the case in other instances, or to engage the richness of the human imagination simply because it is there. To read the Bible solely as a source for theology or ethics or history (or as any other kind of "source" for that matter) is to go to it in order to extract information that one can take away. Having done so, there is no need to go back to it. But to read the Bible as literature is to pay attention to precisely those qualities that do more than communicate information, those qualities of linguistic imagining that may startle and provoke, or soothe and comfort, or perhaps just ask us to enjoy the play of language itself, because we can. And rather than giving us something to "take away" from the Bible, we may well be drawn back to it again and again, since stories and poems tend to withhold some of their favors for repeated visits.

If these ancient Israelite authors had wanted only to tell readers something about God or ethics or history, they did not have to write stories and poems, and they certainly did not have to craft those stories and poems into genuine, subtle examples of literary art. But this is what they did—not always, but often enough that we can reclaim the Bible as a classic of world literature, which both deserves and rewards close, literary attention. In the long run, perhaps such close attention does more than help us see more profoundly the intricate workings of biblical literature since, as the poet Mary Karr has put it, "the mere exercise of attention— eyes wide, ears pricked, heart open—is not a bad way to move through the world."

Chapter 1
Biblical literature and the Western literary tradition

It is hard to deny that in many respects the Hebrew Bible is among the most "unliterary" works of literature that we have. Nor is this judgment entirely attributable to the mass of legal material one encounters, to "getting bogged down in Leviticus" as the phrase so often goes. For even those portions of the Bible made up of classical Hebrew narrative (most of Genesis, the first half of Exodus, the books of Samuel) exhibit a style that often seems simple, even primitive, in comparison with great works of world literature from the *Iliad* and the *Odyssey* to the *Tale of Genji* to *Lolita*.

For example, biblical narrative works with a very limited vocabulary, and it often repeats a word several times rather than resorting to synonyms. Its syntax also seems rudimentary to modern ears, linking clause after clause with a simple "and" that reveals little about their syntactical relationship (a system linguists call "parataxis") instead of using complex sentences with subordinate clauses ("hypotaxis"). The dogged repetition of the word "face" and the run-on syntax in the following very literal translation of Genesis 32:21 (where Jacob is sending ahead of him a very large gift to his estranged brother Esau, in hopes that Esau will be placated over Jacob's earlier stealing of his blessing): "For he said, 'Let me cover his face with the gift that goes before my face and after I look upon his face perhaps he will lift up my face.'"

To a modern reader the sentence sounds stilted, to say the least, but it is not untypical for biblical narrative. And if modern translations tend to obscure these features of syntax and vocabulary, even when one is not reading the Hebrew one is bound to notice the meagerness of metaphorical description, the brevity of dialogue, the lack of reference to the interior lives of characters, the limited use of figural perspective (that is, switching to the point of view of characters in the narrative), and not least the jarring concreteness with which God is imagined to be involved in human history.

The Bible's economy of style

Many of these features are elements of biblical literature's rigorous economy of style. Biblical literary style, especially in its narrative mode, is extraordinarily understated, almost minimalist. Readers are given a bare minimum of information, and linguistic ornamentation for its own sake is noticeably lacking. Compare, for example, Homer's characteristic practice, in the ancient Greek epics the *Iliad* and the *Odyssey*, of using vivid and sometimes startling metaphors in describing a scene with the practice of biblical authors, who by and large avoid such elaborate figurative language. Here, from Homer's *Iliad*, is a description of the death of a single, obscure Trojan charioteer:

> Patroclus rising beside him stabbed his right jawbone,
> ramming the spearhead square between his teeth so hard he
> hooked him by that spearhead over the chariot-rail, hoisted,
> dragged the Trojan out as an angler perched on a
> jutting rock ledge drags some fish from the sea, some
> noble catch, with line and glittering bronze hook.

This is very different from the blunt recounting in Genesis 34:25–26 of the massacre of an entire city by two of Jacob's sons: "Simeon and Levi, Dinah's brothers, took their swords and came against the city unawares, and killed all the men. They killed Hamor and his son Shechem with the sword."

Indeed, it is not just that biblical narrative makes scant use of metaphors but that it tends to avoid description of any sort, metaphorical or otherwise. The principle applies, with some exceptions of course, not only to physical description—so that we are rarely told what either objects or people look like—but also, and more importantly, to the inner lives, thoughts, and motivations of characters in the narratives. It would be a mistake, however, to take this economy of style as an indicator of the Bible's simplicity or primitiveness as a work of literature. In fact, it is in no small part this terseness that lends biblical narrative its distinctive complexity as literature.

Speaking of the Bible's "distinctive complexity as literature" is to foreground both the *distinctiveness* of the Bible and its recognizable status as *literature*. To read the Bible as literature, then, is to look for and interpret those features of its narrative and poetry that it shares with other nonbiblical narrative and poetry. By so doing we may begin to see the Bible's place in the Western literary tradition and not just religious tradition. At the same time, we can look for features that are distinctive to biblical literature. This is not to claim that biblical literature, simply because it is in the Bible, is somehow unique, but rather to recognize that although there are certain genres and categories that can cut across cultures and historical periods, particular examples of literature are always culturally and historically specific. In beginning to practice reading the Bible as literature, we will want to pay attention to the ways in which biblical literature exhibits characteristics typical of narrative and poetry in general, and to the ways in which it offers a distinctive spin on these basic literary categories.

Tragically heroic men and the women who love them: a test case

Near the end of Homer's *Iliad*—in Book 22, after the Greeks and the Trojans have been at war for almost a decade outside the besieged city of Troy—comes the death of Hector (the Trojan champion) at the hands of Achilles (the champion of the Greeks).

> …as Hector charged in fury brilliant Achilles drove his spear
> and the point went stabbing clean through the tender neck…
> …The end closed in around him,
> flying free of his limbs
> his soul went winging down to the House of Death,
> wailing his fate, leaving his manhood far behind,
> his young and supple strength.

Hector's father, King Priam, and his mother, Hecuba, watch from the city walls as Achilles, "bent on outrage, on shaming noble Hector," drags the corpse behind his chariot. The emotional tenor of the scene is heightened as the poem recounts the anguished response of father and mother, devoting (in the Greek) fourteen lines to Priam and seven lines to Hecuba. But clearly the emotional climax of Book 22, where the reader feels the impact of Hector's death, comes when the scene shifts to Hector's wife, Andromache, to whom are devoted nearly eighty lines of poetry as she first realizes and then laments the death of Hector.

Andromache, "weaving at her loom, deep in the dark halls," at first has no inkling of the events outside the city wall. Planning for Hector's return from battle—for he has always returned before, why not this time as well?—she calls to her serving-women to prepare for the hero a steaming hot bath. But hearing the wails of grief coming from the walls, she begins to suspect the worst:

> what if great Achilles
> has cut my Hector off from the city, daring Hector,
> and driven him out across the plain, and all alone?—
> He may have put an end to that fatal headstrong pride
> that always seized my Hector…

Andromache is propelled by this thought, "her heart racing, her women close behind," to the ramparts, from which vantage point she witnesses the "ruthless work" of Achilles as he desecrates Hector's corpse. Book 22 closes with Andromache keening a lament over the death of Hector and over the imagined fate of herself and her small child.

This scene from the *Iliad* gives us all the elements of a recognizable "type-scene," that is, a scene that recurs many times in literature or popular culture and which always displays a handful of common elements. The classic example in Homer is the "arming scene," where a warrior is described as preparing for battle by donning the traditional armor and weapons in a traditional, fixed order. In popular culture we might think of the inevitable gunfight scene in every American Western, or the scene in every Hollywood romantic comedy where the couple "meet cute." The type-scene here in Book 22 of the *Iliad* is one in which women are portrayed as waiting, in vain, for their men to return from war. (In recent memory, Steven Spielberg's movie *Saving Private Ryan* made use of just this type-scene in order to justify the expedition to save Private Ryan, whose mother has received the news of the deaths of her other sons.)

Here are the basic elements of the scene: First, the *violent death* of a male warrior. Second, the women are fundamentally *passive*: they wait, and they react. Third, the place of waiting for the women, especially for Andromache in this case, is clearly identified as *the domestic realm* with all its comforts ("And she called to her well-kempt woman through the house / to set a large three-legged cauldron over the fire / so Hector could have his steaming hot bath / when he came home from battle."), which contrasts with the brutal male realm of combat ("poor woman, / she never dreamed how far he was from bathing, / stuck down at Achilles' hands"). Fourth, in this domestic realm there are hints, although rarely more than hints, of a *female solidarity*, a counterpart of sorts to the more celebrated male solidarity in battle. So the poetry moves from Andromache calling to her serving-women to prepare the hot bath for Hector to the final line of Book 22: "Her voice rang out in tears and the women wailed in answer." Fifth, and perhaps most importantly for the type-scene, *motherhood* is invoked to great effect. Thus, Hector is not just a warrior or a casualty of war, but he is also a mother's son: "noble Hecuba / led the wives of Troy in a throbbing chant of sorrow: / 'O my child—my desolation! How can I go on living?'" Likewise, Andromache's grief is deepest when she considers the fate of their child Astyanax: "the boy only a baby, / the son we bore together,... Now what suffering, now he's lost his father." Over half the lines of her voiced lament are devoted to Astyanax.

Now let us compare this scene from the *Iliad* with a passage from the Bible, one that shares the basic elements of the type-scene. The passage quoted below is from the book of Judges, chapter 5, and is a poetic celebration of the death of Sisera, chariot commander of Israel's archenemies the Canaanites, at the hands of a woman named Jael. The previous chapter of Judges recounts Israel's defeat of the Canaanite army, with Sisera fleeing the battlefield on foot and arriving at the tent of Jael, and in that chapter a prose version is given. But here it is in verse form:

> Most blessed of women be Jael,
>> the wife of Heber the Kenite,
>> of tent-dwelling women most blessed.
> He asked water and she gave him milk,
>> she brought him curds in a lordly bowl.
> She put her hand to the tent peg
>> and her right hand to the workmen's mallet;
> she struck Sisera a blow,
>> she crushed his head,
>> she shattered and pierced his temple.
> He sank, he fell,
>> he lay still between her legs;
> between her legs he sank, he fell;
>> where he sank, there he fell, destroyed.

Out of the window she peered,
    the mother of Sisera gazed through the lattice:
"Why is his chariot so long in coming?
    Why tarry the hoofbeats of his chariots?"
Her wisest ladies make answer,
    indeed, she answers the question herself:
"Are they not finding and dividing the spoil?—
    A womb or two per man, per hero;
spoil of dyed stuffs for Sisera,
    spoil of dyed stuffs embroidered,
two pieces of dyed work
    embroidered for my neck as spoil?"

So perish all your enemies, O LORD!
    But your friends—like the sun rising in its might.
                (Judg. 5:24–31, NRSV, slightly modified)

All the elements of our type-scene are here: The violent death of
a male warrior (in this case Sisera); the presence of a woman
(Sisera's mother) waiting at home for news from the battle; the
contrast between the domestic realm associated with women (both
Jael in her tent with milk and curds, and Sisera's mother gazing
out the window of her house) and the male realm of war; the hint
of a female solidarity in the midst of the domestic realm (here as in
the *Iliad* taking the form of serving-women who surround and
respond to their mistress); the importance of motherhood in
establishing a female character's relationship to the slain man.

If the elements we saw in Homer are present in this biblical poem,
how drastically they have been transformed! The focus is on the
death of male warrior, but as commander of the Canaanite troops he
is hardly meant to be a hero to the reader. His death comes not on
the battlefield but pointedly in the domestic realm (the tent of Jael,
with milk and curds at hand), and he is killed not by a stronger,
fiercer warrior but by a woman (who is anything but passive).

Most striking about the scene, however, is the abrupt shift in setting from Jael's tent, where Sisera has just been violently and gruesomely dispatched, to the home of Sisera's mother, who wonders why her son is so late in returning from the battle. Does she, like Andromache, begin to doubt that the man for whom she waits will return from battle after all? If so, then the deeply ironic answer she gives to her own questions—that Sisera is delayed because he and his soldiers are each taking "a womb or two" as spoil, in addition to the elaborate dyed and embroidered cloth that will be brought home to the women who loyally wait—is wishful thinking, a desperate last hope to forestall the onset of grief. But if she has not yet begun to doubt Sisera's return, then we are left with a mother living in a counterfactual world, where a murdered son is still imagined to be alive and is expected home at any minute. In either case, the poignancy of the scene is acute, and the reader cannot help but feel sympathy for this newly sonless mother.

What makes the biblical poem so enthralling, and indeed virtually unprecedented, is the way the poet employs a type-scene that elicits the sympathy of the reader; this sympathy is elicited, however, not on behalf of a beloved hero and his bereaved mother but instead on behalf of the enemy and the enemy's mother. The poem is not by any means free of pro-Israelite propaganda, as we see in its final, triumphalistic line. And if on first reading one cannot help but feel for Sisera's mother, on second reading one cannot help but balk at the coarseness with which she imagines the fate of the Israelite girls that, ostensibly, Sisera and his soldiers are off raping before they come home for their hot baths. These girls warrant only a half-line of thought before she moves to imagine in much more detail her share in the spoil. But the sympathy elicited by the first reading is surely not entirely supplanted by the moral reprobation elicited by the second. The result is a richly imagined, morally ambivalent perspective on the world, a perspective that the poet achieves by both using and transforming the elements of the type-scene.

"Fraught with background"

Much of what is interesting about the story of Sisera's death is to be found in details particular to this story, especially in the way it plays on and reverses the reader's expectations and sympathies. But we can also take it as a general example of how biblical literature works, in the first place as narrative and then as poetry.

In the opening chapter of his book *Mimesis*, the twentieth-century scholar of comparative literature Erich Auerbach offered the first and best modern articulation of how the drastic terseness of biblical narrative, which he contrasts with Homer, is not just the absence of style but is in fact a distinctive and profound literary mode in its own right. Auerbach describes Homeric style as being "of the foreground," whereas biblical narratives are by contrast "fraught with background." In other words, in the *Iliad* and the *Odyssey* both objects and persons tend to be fully described and illuminated, with essential attributes and aspects—from physical descriptions to the thoughts and motivations of characters—there in the foreground for the reader to see.

But with biblical narrative such details are, for the most part, kept in the background and are not directly available to the reader. What do Adam and Eve look like? We do not know. Abraham? Sarah? Moses? We do not know. As Auerbach puts it in his comments on Genesis 22, where God commands Abraham to sacrifice his son Isaac, it is unthinkable that the servants, the landscape, the implements of sacrifice should be described or praised, as one might expect in Homer: "they are serving-men, ass, wood, and knife, and nothing else, without an epithet." Occasionally a certain quality is ascribed to some person or object: we are told that Eve perceives that the tree of knowledge is "lovely to look at" (Gen. 3:6), and likewise we are told that Joseph is "comely in features and comely to look at" (Gen. 39:6). But as a rule such minimal notations are given only when necessary to introduce some element that is important to the development of the plot. The attractiveness of the tree of knowledge leads, of course, to the eating of its fruit. (But what kind of fruit? We are not told, the long tradition of the apple notwithstanding.) Joseph's attractiveness leads to the sexual aggression of Potiphar's wife and thus indirectly to Joseph's imprisonment. And even in these cases, the reader is not told what it is that makes the fruit lovely to look at or what exactly makes Joseph so beautiful.

Beyond a lack of physical description in the biblical stories, descriptions of personal qualities are largely left unstated as well. That is, characterization is rarely explicit but must be teased out of the narrative based on what characters do and say. By not directly revealing the qualities of character of the actors in the narrative, the narrator puts the onus of interpretation on the readers, who must work out on their own—albeit with hints given—what they think of these characters. This is not the *absence* of characterization but is a certain mode of characterization, and in fact a fairly complex mode at that.

How does biblical narrative's characteristic economy of style play out in the story of Jael and Sisera? Although our passage from Judges 5 is not typical of biblical narrative in that it is in poetic or verse form (whereas most biblical narrative is in prose), there are enough narrative elements in the poetic version of the scene to proceed, especially if we add to our analysis the prose version of the scene found in Judges 4:17–22:

> Now Sisera had fled away on foot to the tent of Jael wife of Heber the Kenite; for there was peace between King Jabin of Hazor and the clan of Heber the Kenite. Jael came out to meet Sisera, and said to him, "Turn aside, my lord, turn aside to me; have no fear." So he turned aside to her into the tent, and she covered him with a rug. Then he said to her, "Please give me a little water to drink; for I am thirsty." So she opened a skin of milk and gave him a drink and covered him. He said to her, "Stand at the entrance of the tent, and if anybody comes and asks you, 'Is anyone here?' say, 'No.'" But Jael

wife of Heber took a tent peg, and took a hammer in her hand, and went softly to him and drove the peg into his temple, until it went down into the ground—he was lying fast asleep from weariness—and he died. Then, as Barak came in pursuit of Sisera, Jael went out to meet him, and said to him, "Come, and I will show you the man whom you are seeking." So he went into her tent; and there was Sisera lying dead, with the tent peg in his temple.

Let's begin with the question of *why* Jael kills Sisera. There is no obviously right answer. Some readers take Jael to be motivated by either religious duty or national interest—that is, she kills Sisera because he is an enemy of Israel or an enemy of Israel's god. But the story does not state either of these motivations, and there are indications that things are possibly more complicated.

In the first place, Jael is not an Israelite but a Kenite, and we are given no indication that she holds some hidden loyalty to either Israel or to Israel's god. What other motivations might she have for killing Sisera? One obvious possibility is that alone in her tent with this man of war, she is concerned for her own personal safety. Though obviously exhausted by the battle, who knows what he might be capable of once his strength is restored. So, we can imagine Jael taking the opportunity to dispatch Sisera before he has the chance to do anything to her. And this theme of soldiers assaulting civilian women is, of course, foregrounded by the comments of Sisera's mother in Judges 5:30 ("A womb or two"), so it is on the immediate horizon of our text.

Another good possibility is that Jael is concerned not so much with her own personal safety but with the survival of her household. Or another way to put it would be that she is not afraid of Sisera himself but of the Israelite army that is in hot pursuit of him and may well arrive at any moment. According to this reading, Jael sees Sisera the chariot commander arriving alone, without his chariot, and much the worse for wear from the battle. Readers know that her husband has chosen the wrong side in this war (Judg. 4:17 "Peace between King Jabin of Hazor and the clan of Heber the Kenite"), and we can imagine Jael realizing that Sisera has been soundly defeated, and that if the Israelite army arrives and finds him hiding here, it will go badly for Jael and her household. So perhaps this is a chance to get on the right side before it is too late. As events unfold, Barak and the Israelites do arrive at Jael's tent in search of Sisera, and instead of having to risk hiding their enemy—and after all, how many good hiding places can there be in a tent?—Jael can announce that she has killed him for them (something they were unable to do).

We could probably come up with other possible motivations for Jael's killing of Sisera, but these are enough to illustrate the extent to which unspoken and unrevealed thoughts and feelings that drive the action of the story in a way typical of biblical narrative. We also do not know what Barak is thinking when Jael reveals the dead Sisera to him. Is it relief that this enemy has been killed? Shame at not having killed Sisera himself? (Compare Deborah's prediction in Judg. 4:9 that Barak will get no glory from the battle.) Distrust of Jael, whose husband after all has sided with Sisera and the Canaanites? And we do not know what is really going through the mind of Sisera's mother, who may or may not have begun to suspect that her son is not returning from battle this time. And this makes a difference for how we as readers react to her, since her coarse comment about how the soldiers must be off raping a few Israelite girls is mitigated somewhat if we hear it as the desperate statement of an anxiety-filled mother rather than the glib comment of an unfeeling and self-assured member of the ruling class. The point is that it can easily be read as either of these, and the uncertainty—the "background" that is not revealed to the reader—adds a layer of complexity to the story.

What makes biblical poetry "poetry"?

The twentieth-century poet and critic T. S. Eliot once wrote that "When we are considering poetry we must consider it primarily as poetry and not another thing." This is sensible advice, and not nearly as obvious as it might seem at first blush. For one thing, it is not always easy to determine what makes "poetry," given any number of definitions of the term. For another, it is not entirely clear what constitutes considering a text *as poetry*; in any case it is clear that interpreters of the Bible have tended to consider biblical poetry *as another thing*, traditionally as theological statements but more recently as sources of history or even, mistakenly, as narratives. Now, let's see how Eliot's dictum might help us become good readers of biblical poetry.

If you pick up a Bible today, you will see that a large portion of the text is presented as poetry, or verse. That is, about a third of the Hebrew Bible is "lineated"—set off in lines that stop before getting to the margin of the page. This is of course the most basic definition of poetry, strictly defined as verse in distinction from prose. When one writes prose one just keeps writing until reaching the margin, whereas the poet will stop writing and move to the next line even if there is room to write more. This is why there is generally quite a bit of white space surrounding the text in a book of poetry, rather than the page-filling blocks of text one sees in, for example, a novel. The question then becomes what principle, if any, exists for knowing when to stop the line.

In much poetry of the Western literary tradition—ancient Greek and Roman poetry and most English poetry up until the last hundred years or so—the length of the line is determined by meter, or an established pattern of stressed and unstressed syllables. In the most well-known type of line in English poetry, iambic pentameter, one knows that there will be an alternation of five unstressed and five stressed syllables, as in the following line from Shakespeare's Sonnet 12 (with stressed words capitalized): "When I do COUNT the CLOCK that TELLS the TIME." When the given pattern of stressed syllables runs out, the line reaches its end. Meter is often combined with rhyme in English (and other) poetry, as in this line of William Blake's: "Tyger, Tyger, burning *bright,* / in the forests of the *night.*" In such a case, the line ending is cinched by the rhyme.

But in ancient Hebrew poetry neither meter nor rhyme were determining factors in the poetic line. The question of what makes biblical poetry "poetry" is still a matter of some debate. And it would seem to be the case that for many centuries the basic principles of ancient Hebrew poetry went largely if not entirely unrecognized, or at least uncommented upon. Thus while nearly all Bibles printed today will represent in verse form the book of Psalms, the book of Job, the Song of Songs, and the book of Proverbs, as well as several major poems embedded in prose narratives (e.g., passages in Judg. 5; Ex 15; 2 Sam. 1; and Deut. 32), Before the mid-twentieth century Bibles represented these texts as blocks of prose. But in the late eighteenth century biblical poetry underwent a sort of "rediscovery," especially associated with the work of Robert Lowth's *Lectures on the Sacred Poetry of the Hebrews,* which introduced the term "parallelism" to describe the primary structuring principle of the ancient Hebrew poetic line.

Biblical scholars have tended to follow Lowth in referring to the most basic building block of ancient Hebrew poetry as "parallelism," in which two short lines (sometimes called "cola" or "versets") are put in parallel position to one another, with the occasional third short line or verset added. The resulting "couplet" (or occasional "triplet") form is what tells us in the Hebrew Bible that we are in the presence of poetry or verse, rather than prose. Since Lowth's programmatic treatment of this phenomenon of parallelism in the eighteenth century, scholars have tended to see the relationship between the lines as automatic, with the second line functioning as a reflexive restatement of the first. But recent work on ancient Hebrew poetry has shown that poets worked with a great deal of freedom in articulating the poetic lines, and that the relationship between lines is much more subtle and dynamic than previous treatments of "parallelism" had indicated. In particular, whereas it was once thought that the second line essentially said the same thing in different words, it has become clear that it will often move beyond the language or imagery in the first line by making it more concrete, focused, or specific, or more intense or emotionally heightened. The second (or third) line will sometimes also represent a chronological progression or a sort of miniature narrative development of the first line.

But for most of us, putting something in verse form is not enough to really qualify it as poetry in the broader sense. For example, the phone book is in "verse" form, in the sense that it is lined out on the page, with clear markers as to where one line ends and another begins, but we would not call the phone book "poetry" (unless to make a mischievous point about the nature of poetry). Similarly, there are two lists of names in the Bible, found in Joshua 12:9–11 and Esther 9:7–9, that are sometimes set off as lines in Hebrew manuscripts, but no one seems to want to identify these lists as poetry.

What is it that makes poetry then? The literary theorist Terry Eagleton argues that poetry must not only be in verse form but must also be "moral" and "fictional." By *moral*, he does not mean that it teaches the reader lessons on good or bad per se, but that it is concerned with larger questions about human behavior, human welfare, and the purposes and meaning of life. He contrasts moral with empirical, the latter meaning a concern with stating facts or with giving information. But poetry, as a subspecies of literature, wants to go beyond such practical concerns in order to make a claim about the very nature of human existence—or if that sounds too grandiose (and I admit that it might) then we could say that poetry wants to evoke a feeling, or stir up a thought or two, or even just entertain or impress the reader. By *fictional*, Eagleton means a piece of writing detached from any immediate and practical context. It is not tied to a certain, specific context but has been unmoored so as to be taken up by readers in very different contexts than the one in which it was written. One need not have been there with Wordsworth when he saw his daffodils in order to appreciate his poem about daffodils; indeed it does not matter whether Wordsworth ever in fact saw a daffodil in his life in order for his poem about them to affect a reader.

One does not want to be too loose perhaps in these matters of context and poet biography. It may make a difference in interpreting, say, Anna Akhmatova's poems about living in Stalinist Russia if the reader discovers Akhmatova did not in fact live through the hardships she alludes to. (For the record, she did.) And Paul Celan's poems about the Holocaust might sound different to a reader if he or she were to discover they were written by a white, Anglo-Saxon Protestant born in the United States in 1965. (For the record, they were not.) The point is that whether or not the poem can be tied to an author's specific historical and factual context—and the extent to which it can be is not irrelevant—it has nevertheless been unmoored from that context in order to be available to readers in other contexts. "To call something a poem," Eagleton writes, "is to put it into general circulation, as one wouldn't do with one's laundry list."

To take a biblical example, the poem found in Psalm 22 begins with the plaintive question, "My God, my God, why have you forsaken me?" We know very little indeed about the person who wrote this poem and whether they felt personally forsaken by God. It is entirely possible that the author did have such feelings, and that he or she expressed them directly in this poem. But it is equally if not more likely that the author was a professional poet who wrote this poem for liturgical use in the ancient Temple in Jerusalem. In either case, its status *as a poem* depends not on the putative experience of the author but rather on the experience of the reader or, in a liturgical context, we might say the reciter of the poem. The ability of this particular poem to be unmoored from its context and reused in another was famously demonstrated when the author of the Gospel of Mark put this first line into the mouth of Jesus on the cross. It is a powerful and moving moment in Mark's gospel, because we can imagine Jesus expressing his very real pain by means of this poem that might have been familiar to him. At the same time, Mark's gospel might also be considered "fictional" in that it does not matter whether Jesus actually spoke these words from the cross in order for the words to work very well at that point in the narrative.

"Not another thing"

What would it mean then to take T. S. Eliot's advice about considering poetry as poetry and apply it to biblical poetry? First, it means paying attention to the formal elements that mark a biblical passage as verse. This includes the varieties of line structure that we encounter, where it is always worth asking how the second or third lines relate to the first, whether as a form of parallelism or something else, as well as other formal markers of Hebrew verse. By paying attention to such poetic elements, we are honoring the *craft* of poetry, the effort by ancient authors to shape this literature in a very specific way and with very specific results.

In the second place, it means asking about the "moral" and/or "fictional" qualities of the literature, or the ways in which the poetry does more than just communicate information to the reader. Can the poetry still come alive in some way for later readers? Does it address issues that are of perennial interest? Or maybe even just the question of whether there might be a line or two that is memorable enough to help in furnishing our mental or emotional landscape. The author of the gospel of Mark found that Psalm 22 resonated with how he or she wanted to shape the scene of Jesus's final suffering and death. The poet Gerard Manley Hopkins no doubt found inspiration in Psalm 8 as he worked to express in sonnet form a vision of God's presence in creation, coming up with the opening line "The world is charged with the grandeur of God." And we might find that reading and thinking about the poem celebrating Sisera's death at the hands of Jael pushes us to consider such moral issues as the fate of women in war, the sending of soldiers into battle, or the question of at what point poetry veers into nationalist propaganda.

In the third place, considering biblical poetry as poetry and not as another thing means paying attention to the function of verse in biblical literature, to how it gets used. This is important because verse is used for different purposes, for different literary genres, than is prose. Most strikingly, ancient Israel, unlike virtually all other peoples of the ancient Near East, did not use poetry for the telling of long stories, preferring prose for that task. Verse in the Bible, then, is almost exclusively nonnarrative. It was very unusual to find, in the story of Jael and Sisera, a biblical narrative in verse form. There is no denying that the poetry in Judges 5 contains the basic elements of narrative: characters (Jael, Sisera, Sisera's mother), plot tension (How will Jael respond to Sisera? What will be the fate of Sisera's mother?), and action (Jael's memorable wielding of the tent peg). But this passage is one of the very few exceptions that prove the rule, with the Song of Moses in Exodus 15 being another example of verse narrative in the Bible. But we may notice that each of these counterexamples is very brief, confirming that for *extended* narrative in the Bible, prose is used exclusively. Moreover, neither of these brief narrative runs really exists in order to tell a story, but instead serves to evoke an emotional response, to celebrate in song a story that the audience already knows in each case from the surrounding prose narratives. And this task—the expressing and evoking of emotion—is one to which biblical poetry is well suited and in fact, unlike biblical prose narrative, revels in.

To read the Bible "as literature," then, means paying attention to its two primary and distinctive literary modes of narrative and poetry. The two modes are quite consistently distinguished by both form and function, using different literary tools toward different ends. Both of these literary modes reward close reading, and both will require more in-depth description and engagement.

Chapter 2
Reading biblical narrative

Some two and a half or three thousand years ago a group of writers in ancient Israel invented the novel. This assertion flies in the face of the standard histories of the novel, which typically claim *Don Quixote* (from early seventeenth-century Spain) as the first real example. Sometimes the invention of the novel will be pushed back to the Icelandic sagas of the thirteenth century, or even further to *The Tale of Genji*, from eleventh-century Japan. It is probably best to say, as Jane Smiley does in her book *13 Ways of Looking at the Novel*, that the novel was invented many times. And the truth is that all the essential, defining elements of the novel are present already in the Bible. A novel is a written, prose narrative, sufficiently *long* that it probably cannot be read in a single sitting, which develops a *plot* that drives the story and *characters* that show signs of a genuine and complex inner life. All of these elements are necessary to a novel, and all can be found in biblical literature, most especially perhaps in the books of Genesis and of 1 and 2 Samuel.

In addition to these examples of long narratives, biblical literature also preserves ancient versions of what we might think of as short stories. A short story is like a novel in many respects—except, of course, a good bit shorter. Unlike the novel, the short story can and should be read in one sitting. Its impact depends less on tracking the complex and shifting development of plot and character, and more on its ability to represent a particular fraught moment in the lives of its characters. These characters, although not given the chance to develop over time in the same way as characters in the more leisurely paced novel, can nevertheless potentially display a similar complexity and depth of characterization. Our two primary examples of short stories in the Bible are the book of Ruth and the book of Esther.

One may finally disagree that narratives we find in the Bible should be thought of as novels or short stories, and indeed I would not want to push that point too hard. Admittedly, the physical form of the novel as a book between covers and the way in which it can be mass-produced and consumed, which would not be true of ancient literature, contributes much to our notion of what constitutes a novel. Yet by exploring the workings of biblical narrative, with examples from both its long and short forms, we can bring into focus those elements that make us feel that we are reading literature and not just straightforward theology, or ethics, or a historical recounting of events.

More important than coming up with a label for these biblical narratives is to see that they display not only many of the basic elements that we associate with literary works but also, as I will hope to show, the deftness of touch that characterizes good fictional narrative. Is this to claim then that the Bible is, in the end, *fiction*? No—at least not in the popular sense of fiction as something essentially untrue. Clearly there is much in biblical narrative that is not factually true, but there is also probably much that is factually true. Our question here is not whether the narratives are true in the sense of representing something that really happened, but rather how these narratives exhibit—often in complex and sophisticated ways—the features of fictional narrative literature.

How fiction (and the Bible) works

In his book *How Fiction Works*, the literary critic James Wood identifies two things as particularly characteristic of novelistic fiction. The first of these is what he calls "thisness." "By thisness," Wood writes, "I mean any detail that draws abstraction towards itself and seems to kill that abstraction with a puff of palpability, any detail that centers our attention with its concretion." Beginning in the eighteenth-century novel, the description of seemingly insignificant details—the pungent smell of a character's cigar, the wax picked up from the dance floor by a pair of slippers, the greasiness of a minor character's hair—lends an aura of realism to fictional narrative. The inconsequentiality of such details (they do not really advance the plot, nor do they always contribute to characterization) constitutes, paradoxically, their significance for readers, since they are there in the story only to evoke the real world of our experience, which is of course filled with insignificant details. Such realism is one of the markers of the emergence of the modern novel, setting it apart from less realistic ancient and medieval narratives. (Though the novel eventually expands beyond such a realist mode, as fantasy, science fiction, and "magical realist" novels proliferate.)

The Bible tends not to trade much in the "thisness" of detail, rarely describing either objects or characters and including very little in the way of detail that is not strictly necessary to the plot. This general lack of detail, combined with the general lack of metaphor in biblical narrative (though not in biblical poetry), has contributed to a common misperception that biblical literature is essentially artless. But this tendency of the Bible should not be mistaken for the *absence* of style, but should be recognized as a *particular* style, one that pushes the reader's attentions from the foreground, where such details might be described and where character motivation might be made explicit, to the background, where objects are dimly perceived and motivations left unexpressed.

However, the sparing use of detail in biblical narrative also means that when we do encounter it, we ought to pay close attention, since such detail is almost never gratuitous but instead reveals something especially important about a particular character or, perhaps, foreshadows some aspect of the plot. For example, when David is first introduced into the narrative of 1 Samuel, we are told that he is "ruddy and handsome, with beautiful eyes" (1 Sam. 16:12). The brief description foregrounds David's charismatic appeal and presages his great success in winning over the loyalty of the people. The adjective "beautiful" is slightly—but only slightly—feminizing, and helps to explain why it is that both men and women are perpetually falling in love with David. Only two other male characters in biblical narrative are described with this particular term for beauty: Joseph (in Gen. 39:6) and David's son Absalom (in 2 Sam. 14:25). Again, the descriptions are not gratuitous. Joseph's beauty leads directly to the unwanted sexual advances of Potiphar's wife and to his imprisonment and, indirectly, to his eventual elevation as viceroy in Egypt, from which position he is eventually able to save his family during a severe famine and thus ensure the survival of the people of Israel (see Gen. 39–50 for the whole story). It is not too much to say that according to the plot of Genesis, if it were not for Joseph's beauty there would be no Israel. Hardly a gratuitous detail, then.

With Absalom, there is real irony in the fact that he has inherited his father's unusual beauty, since he uses that beauty to "steal the hearts of the people of Israel" away from David, eventually mounting a rebellion against his father and usurping the throne. Absalom's beauty is associated especially with his extravagantly full head of hair, which, we are told by the narrator in an unusually specific detail, he cuts only once a year, and when he does so the weight of the hair is "two hundred shekels [about six pounds] by the king's weight" (2 Sam. 14:26). Though initially successful in his rebellion, Absalom's time as king is short-lived, for not long afterward his army is defeated by those loyal to David, and Absalom himself suffers an inglorious death. How is he killed? His luxurious hair is caught in the branches of a tree as he rides underneath, and he is left hanging helpless, to be killed ruthlessly by David's general Joab (2 Sam. 18:9–15). The seemingly

unnecessary detail of Absalom's beautiful hair, then, both alerts
the reader to the source of his charismatic authority and presages
his eventual downfall.

If Hebrew biblical narrative tends to make sparing use of detail,
and so does not display "thisness" in the same pervasive way that
the novel does, its ability to hint at unexpressed thoughts, feelings,
and motivations on the part of its characters is one of the things
that make it most comparable to the novel. For, as Wood points
out in a chapter titled "A Brief History of Consciousness," the
second primary hallmark of the modern novel is the
representation of psychological complexity, of "deep, self-divided
characters." Though often read as presenting characters that are
solely concerned with God and motivated only by piety, one of the
most distinctive aspects of biblical narrative is the way in which it
exploits to good effect a genuinely private self in its characters,
one that is largely inaccessible to readers and to other characters.
We have seen that biblical narrative consistently, but not slavishly,
avoids giving access to the inner lives of its characters, to what
they might be thinking or feeling in any given situation, even
though that inner life is often vitally important to character
motivation and to plot development, and it cannot always be
filled in with reference to God.

It is easy to mistake the reader's lack of access to characters' inner
lives for a denial of the existence of such inner lives. But the
literary convention is for the narrator to report action and
dialogue (what the characters do and what they say), and not, for
the most part, what they think or feel. So, when Wood writes
about King David's sexual taking of Bathsheba that "he sees and
acts," but that "as far as the narrative is concerned, he does not
think," he is at best only half right. David is indeed reported by the
narrator, in 2 Samuel 11, as seeing from his rooftop Bathsheba
bathing and then acting to bring her into his bed; but the fact that
he is not *reported* as thinking does not mean that the reader
should not *imagine* him as thinking. In fact, the story gives clear

indication that after seeing Bathsheba, David pauses and considers his next action. He sends someone to "inquire about the woman," and he learns that she is "the daughter of Eliam, the wife of Uriah the Hittite." Only after gaining this information does David carry out his act of adultery.

How might this information help us to understand David's thinking here? He learns that this woman's husband, though a member of David's army, is a Hittite and not a native Israelite, and so perhaps we are to understand David as having fewer scruples about taking the wife of a non-Israelite. (There is obvious irony in the fact that, as the story unfolds, Uriah in fact proves a much better keeper than David of Israelite law.) David also learns that Bathsheba is the daughter of Eliam, who in turn, the attentive reader will notice, is the son of Ahitophel, one of the court counselors who a couple of chapters later in the story will betray David by siding with David's son Absalom in his attempted coup. This fact might well lead us to wonder about David's motivation in sleeping with Bathsheba. It would be easy to assume that David acts out of an unthinking lust that wants no other motivation. But in fact the reader is not told that he lusts after Bathsheba. And it is possible to imagine David's taking of Bathsheba as a calculated political act against a rival faction within the court. (The sexual control of women elsewhere in the David story is clearly a political matter.) The point is that we are not privy to David's motivation (or motivations—after all, lust and politics are not mutually exclusive), but he clearly has *some* motivation and is portrayed as calculating options—that is, thinking—before acting.

Examples such as this, in which character motivation is unstated but important and potentially very complicated, abound in biblical narrative. What are Eve and Adam thinking when they reach for the fruit from the tree of the knowledge of good and evil in the garden of Eden? What is God thinking in forbidding that fruit? (Despite Christianity's long tradition of original sin, the answer to neither of these questions is immediately clear, and both prove

32

quite interestingly complex if taken seriously.) Why does Moses kill the Egyptian who is beating a Hebrew slave in Exodus 2:11–12? (It is not clear whether Moses, raised an Egyptian, knows that he was born a Hebrew, and so his motivation might range from an elemental sense of justice, unrelated to ethnicity, to a specifically ethnic identification with the victim.) Why does Naomi try to send Ruth back to her Moabite family in the first chapter of the book of Ruth? (Is she genuinely concerned for Ruth's welfare, or does she simply want to be rid of the burden of a non-Israelite woman as she returns from Moab to Bethlehem.) Why does Queen Vashti refuse the king's order to appear before him and his noblemen in chapter 1 of the book of Esther, thus setting the entire plot of the book in motion? (Is it a simple assertion of her queenly rights? Or a political move? Or, as traditional readings sometime suggest, a function of her modesty in the face of what she takes to be a prurient request on the part of the king?)

As these brief examples show—and there are many, many more that could be given—biblical narrative counts on and exploits exactly that which defines the treatment of character in novelistic fiction: a genuine inner life and a private, complex subjectivity. This represented subjectivity is complex in the sense that it allows for layers of consciousness, which are often in conflict with each other. King Saul, for example, loves the charismatic David who soothes Saul's demons with his lyre playing, even while he hates and fears the David who is destined to take his throne. And David, many years later, will in turn be torn between his love for his son Absalom and the need to put down Absalom's rebellion, leading to one of his most famous (and rare) expressions of feeling, upon hearing of Absalom's death in battle: "O my son Absalom, my son, my son Absalom! Would I had died instead of you, O Absalom, my son, my son!" (3 Sam. 19:4).

Characterization in biblical literature

It is worth thinking more about the inner lives of those who populate biblical narrative, especially in relation to "characterization," or the ways in which authors develop believable (or not believable) characters and convey information to readers about them. Readers of Western literature are used to having access in one form or another to the thoughts, feelings, and motivations of the characters about whom they read. As Auerbach writes of Homer: "With the utmost fullness, with an orderliness which even passion does not disturb, Homer's personages vent their inmost hearts in speech; what they do not say to others, they speak in their own minds, so that the reader is informed of it. Much that is terrible takes place in the Homeric poems, but it seldom takes place wordlessly." And so the tragic death of Hector at the hands of Achilles near the end of the *Iliad* (in Book 22), for example, has devoted to it (in the Greek) fourteen lines of lament by Hector's father, seven lines by his mother, and fully forty lines by his wife Andromache. We may compare this with the brief notations of grief in biblical narrative. On the death of Sarah: "And Sarah died in Kiriath-Arba, which is Hebron, in the land of Canaan, and Abraham came to mourn Sarah and to keen for her" (Gen. 23:2). On the death of Moses: "And the Israelites keened for Moses in the steppes of Moab thirty days, and the days of keening in mourning for Moses came to an end" (Deut. 34:8).

One might object that since both Sarah and Moses had lived long and fruitful lives, their deaths lack the tragedy of noble Hector being cut down in his prime over the affairs of his less-noble brother Paris, and thus inspire less intense expressions of mourning. But even with more obviously tragic deaths, we see in biblical narrative the restraint of the narrator, who acknowledges the grief of the survivors but refrains from allowing them full expression of it. Earlier we noted Jacob's response to what he takes to be evidence of his young, beloved son Joseph's death: "A vicious beast has devoured him, / Joseph torn to shreds!" (Gen. 37:33). In a scene that seems intended to characterize Jacob as an extravagant mourner, the narrator goes on to describe Jacob as rending his clothes and donning sackcloth and refusing to be comforted by his other children: "'Rather I will go down to my son in Sheol in mourning,' and his father keened for him" (37:35). Yet even here the few scant lines in Hebrew do not come close to matching the sixty lines of direct lament over the death of Hector, not to mention the extended scene in Book 24 of the *Iliad* where Hector's father Priam goes to the tent of Achilles to beg for the return of his son's much-abused corpse.

Consider also the notoriously ambiguous story in Leviticus 10 of the burning Nadab and Abihu, the sons of Aaron. The reader is told that the two young priests brought "strange fire" or "alien fire" (Hebrew: *'esh zara*) before the Lord, "and fire came out from before the Lord and consumed them, and they died before the Lord" (10:2). Moses very quickly offers a sort of cryptic theodicy, cast as a line of verse, in the face of the shocking event: "This is what the Lord spoke, saying, 'Through those close to Me shall I be hallowed and in all the people's presence shall I be honored'" (10:3).

No more laconic response could be imagined, both to the death of the young men and to Moses's extemporaneous theologizing, than that attributed to Aaron: "And Aaron was silent." Surely we are to imagine Aaron's grief as real and deep—indeed, a few verses later Moses forbids Aaron and his other sons to go through the public rituals of mourning while they are consecrated for service in the temple (10:6–7)—and yet all we are given is his silence, but a silence that demands interpretation. Is Aaron feeling pure shock? Overwhelming sadness? Anger at God? Confusion or despair? Is his silence a rejection of Moses's statement of God's intent? And if so, on what basis? The fact is that we are given no access whatsoever into the inner life of Aaron, and because we do not know what he is thinking, we also do not know what motivates his silence.

It is with regard to this latter issue, the question of character motivation, that we may see the importance of recognizing the distinctively terse mode of biblical narration. As a general rule, the narrator reveals very little about the inner lives of characters, instead reporting mainly action and dialogue, or what the characters *do* and what they *say*. If we are given little or no access to the thoughts and feelings of the characters about whom we read, then it follows that the motivation behind what they do and say is also largely obscure. The importance of this obscurity of motivation can scarcely be overstated for any literary reading of biblical narrative, since this—more than anything else—is what gives the literature its profound complexity as it forces the reader to negotiate the many possible ways of imagining the characters' inner lives.

Genesis 22 and the ambiguities of motivation

In a story that has never failed to engage the imagination of interpreters ancient or modern, God commands Abraham, in Genesis 22, to take his son Isaac and sacrifice him as a burnt offering. Although a few chapters earlier we have seen Abraham challenge the justness of God's decision to destroy Sodom and Gomorrah, here Abraham says nothing in response. Instead, there is the narrator's terse report: "And Abraham rose early in the morning and, saddled his donkey and took his two lads with him, and Isaac his son, and split wood for the offering, and rose and went to the place... that God had said to him. On the third day Abraham raised his eyes and saw the place from afar" (vv. 3–4).

Abraham's silent obedience here is often taken to be motivated by an untroubled and unquestioning faith in God, which depending on one's perspective may be seen, positively, as an expression of ultimate piety or, negatively, as an expression of unfeeling religious fanaticism. But both interpretations fail to recognize the fundamental literary convention of the refusal of access to the inner lives of characters. The fact that we are not told of Abraham's inner, emotional response to the demand that he slaughter his son does not mean that he has no inner, emotional response. I think that we are to assume that he does, but rather than describing it for us or allowing Abraham to give voice to it, the narrator leaves us guessing as to what that response might be and thus also as to his motivation for his actions.

Now, it is possible to fill that gap left by the narrator with an inner calm that reflects absolute faith, but it is equally possible to imagine that Abraham is feeling anger, disbelief, and even disgust (with God for demanding the slaughter? with himself for not protesting?) And however one fills the gap of Abraham's inner life initially, surely it is complicated by Isaac's calling out to him in v. 7, "Father!" and by the plaintive question that follows, "Here is the fire and the wood, but where is the sheep for the offering?" It is precisely because we do not know what Abraham is thinking or feeling that his brief response to Isaac's question takes on a deeply ironic double meaning. On the one hand, it may be read as a ruse, if not an outright lie, to deflect any suspicions that may be dawning on the son; on the other hand, it may be read as a straightforward statement of faith that a sheep will indeed be provided. It may even be the case here that the author makes use of the ambiguities of Hebrew's seemingly rudimentary syntax in order to signal the potential irony to the attentive reader. For there is no punctuation in the Hebrew text, and one may also construe the syntax to read: "God will see to the sheep for the offering: *namely*, my son."

To return to Abraham's initial response to Isaac, we may see how what at first glance looks like wooden repetition may in fact be a subtly modulated use of a key word or theme. When God first calls out to Abraham to begin the episode, Abraham's response is "Here I am" (22:1); when Isaac calls in the middle of the episode, on the way to the place of sacrifice, Abraham's response is, once again, "Here I am, my son" (22:7); and when, at the climactic moment when the knife is raised over the boy, the angel of LORD calls out "Abraham, Abraham!" (22:11) his response is again "Here I am." In each case the single Hebrew word *hinneni*, "here I am" or "behold me," is repeated by Abraham. To substitute a synonym for the sake of variety, as for example the Jewish Publication Society's Tanakh does in translating the second occurrence as "Yes, my son," is to lose a concrete expression of what is certainly a central theme for the story, namely, the anguished tension between the demands of God and the ethical demands of another human being (Abraham's own child no less!).

Surely every ethical impulse demands that Abraham not kill his son, and yet precisely this is what God demands that he do. He responds "Here I am" to both God and Isaac, and yet he cannot be fully "there," fully present, to both equally. It is only with the third, very late, repetition of "Here I am" that the tension is resolved, and Abraham is no longer caught between these opposing demands on his loyalty. One might say that Abraham's threefold response provides the underlying armature for the story, marking the beginning, the middle, and the end. Although the single word *hinneni* is literally repeated each time, it acquires a new depth of meaning—and certainly a new tone—with each repetition. And to the end of the story we are still never quite sure what Abraham is thinking as he first travels in silence, then responds to his son, then binds and raises the knife, and finally sacrifices the ram instead.

If we do not know what motivates Abraham in Genesis 22, it is also the case that we do not know what motivates Isaac to make his inquiry as to the whereabouts of the sheep or what he is thinking as his father binds him and lays him on the makeshift altar. But by this point we are not surprised by this, since we have begun to see that the biblical authors make use of this linguistic convention in order to allow for depth of character and depth of meaning.

It is perhaps somewhat more surprising to note that this convention applies to God too, who is after all a character in these narratives as well, and so the *literary* art of biblical narrative has distinct *theological* implications. What motivates God to demand the sacrifice of Isaac? The narrator refuses to tell us, though for any reader, religious or not, this must certainly be a compelling question. We are told that "God tested Abraham" (22:1), but this does not give us an answer to our question. The sense of the word "test" (Hebrew *nissah*) is something like "trial" or "ordeal," and so God decides to put Abraham through an ordeal, presumably to test his mettle. (A comparison with the opening chapters of Job is apt.) But why, and to what end? Is it to find out how strong Abraham is under pressure? To see whether he values his son more than he values God? Does God genuinely learn something new about Abraham, about humanity, or about God's self through this test? ("Now I know..." [22:12].)

Without knowing what motivates God or what God is thinking as the knife is raised, we cannot finally even know whether Abraham has passed or failed the test. Most readers assume that he has passed, but a few have dared to suggest that God wanted not blind obedience from Abraham but resistance—after all, such resistance was honored when Abraham argued on behalf of Sodom and Gomorrah—and that in failing to argue with God, Abraham failed to show the strength of character that God hoped to see. If such a reading seems strained, especially in light of 22:16 ("because you have done this..."), the fact that it is nonetheless possible—if only just—witnesses to the profound but productive ambiguity of Hebrew literary style, which again exploits to great effect its distinctive economy of style.

Depths of past and future

One of the things that distinguishes biblical literature from virtually all other ancient Near Eastern literature is that its extended narratives take the form of prose and not verse (or poetry). This form is in no small part the effect of a transition from oral composition to written literary art. The traditional oral storyteller, when composing a long narrative, is bound to the strict rhythms of the poetic line. Moreover, because oral composition before a live audience allows little time for pauses, the oral storyteller must be constantly moving forward, always thinking of the next line and the next development in the plot. But the author of a literary text—that is, a text composed by writing—can work at a more leisurely pace, can stop writing and return to the work, and can edit at will. No doubt this change in the means of composition, which is essentially a technical innovation, has much to do with the effects we considered earlier, most especially the ability to build into the story ambiguity and double meanings, and thus expect a reader (as opposed to a listening audience) to catch such subtleties.

But another effect of the transition from orally composed epic poetry (which would include not only the *Iliad* and the *Odyssey*, but the *Epic of Gilgamesh* and other ancient Near Eastern narratives) to a more flexible prose narrative would seem to be the ability to represent the long-term development of characters over the course a lifetime, to show the contours of a lived life, in which the depths of a past both shape and impinge upon the present, which in turn opens out into an uncertain future.

In terms of the latter, the representation of a realistically uncertain future, let's return for a moment to the story of Jael's killing of the Canaanite general Sisera (from Judg. 4 and 5). One aspect of the story that remains unexpressed and largely left in obscurity is the fate of several of the characters. If Jael was trying to reposition her household with regard to the winning side in the war between the Israelites and the Canaanites, as I suggested might be the case, it is not entirely clear that she succeeded in doing do. Although the fact that the victory song of chapter 5 declares Jael to be the "most blessed of women" (v. 24) suggests that she did indeed succeed, her last scene in the story (and in the Bible as a whole) is the scene at the end of chapter 4 when she reveals the murdered Sisera to Barak. The reader is left to wonder what the fate of Jael and her household might be.

Likewise with Sisera's mother, whose future is uncertain as she waits in vain for her son to return from battle. What will happen to Sisera's mother in the long run? We can presume that she will receive the news of his death not long after her scene in chapter 5 closes, and that she will feel the full extent of a mother's grief (which, unlike the similar scene in the *Iliad* where Hector's mother receives the news of his death, considered in the last chapter, is never reported to the reader but only implied). But we may also have hints that a bitterly ironic fate awaits Sisera's mother. As she waits for the sounds of an approaching army—thinking and hoping that it is Sisera returning in triumph—is it too much to imagine that she will indeed hear such an army, but that instead of Sisera it will be the triumphant Israelites coming for the spoils of war?

The poet has raised the issue very explicitly by having Sisera's mother imagine him off collecting spoil and raping women—"Are they not finding and dividing the spoil? A womb or two per man, per hero?"—and are we to imagine that now with the tables reversed she will herself, along with her ladies-in-waiting, become the spoil of their enemies? A careful reader might notice that Barak is encouraged to lead away his "captives" (5:12). Just who are these captives? We know that the entire army of Sisera was put to the sword (4:16), so it is reasonable to assume that these captives are the captured women. We cannot say for sure that this is the fate of Sisera's mother, but that is precisely the stylistic point. That is, biblical narrative style consistently tends to tell stories that are "fraught with background" to give the reader enough detail to tease our imaginations and to elicit our responses, but it withholds enough to leave much of the interpretive work to us.

Biblical narrative's representation of the weight of a lived life over time, and the way in which that shapes a character, may perhaps best be seen in two characters: Jacob in the book of Genesis, and David in the books of Samuel. We first meet Jacob when he is still in the womb of his mother, Rebekah, along with his twin brother Esau, and he is already characterized as a grasper and a striver (Gen. 25:23). Esau emerges from the womb first, thereby securing by a matter of seconds the legal rights of the firstborn son, but quite literally "at his heels" comes Jacob, "his hand gripping Esau's heel" (25:26). We then see Jacob as a young man, first, shrewdly negotiating the birthright from Esau (25:29–34) and, secondly, tricking his father Isaac into giving the formal paternal blessing to him instead of to Esau (ch. 27, a wonderfully rich scene that deserves to be read more closely). Fleeing the understandably angry Esau, Jacob ends up spending years living with his uncle Laban (chs. 28–31), where he eventually tricks Laban out of the best of his flocks, before returning home for a fraught reunion with Esau (ch. 33).

To this point in Jacob's life, then, we have a fairly consistent portrait of a shrewd, not-entirely-honest but very resourceful man, who manages to control most everyone around him toward his own ends. There are a few interesting "blips" in this characterization, one being the very brief notation, "So Jacob served seven years for Rachel [in lieu of a brideprice], and they seemed to him but a few days because of the love he had for her" (29:20). The statement represents an intentional breaking of the general rule against giving access to the inner lives of characters, and the result is to complicate the reader's picture of Jacob, who up to this point we would have no reason to think was capable of genuine love or of self-sacrifice. He is still the same tricky and deceptive Jacob, but have been given a glimpse of a possible other Jacob under the surface.

This other less-controlled and less-controlling Jacob will come to the fore as the narrative continues to trace out his life over two dozen chapters and many years. A breaking point for Jacob would seem to be when his son Joseph (the firstborn of his beloved Rachel) is lost to him: Joseph's brothers, the sons of other mothers, have sold him into slavery in Egypt, though they present his father false evidence indicating that Joseph has been killed by a wild animal (37:20). From this point on, we are clearly dealing with a different Jacob. He can no longer control his family, mourns incessantly for Joseph, and fears for the fate of Benjamin, his only remaining son of Rachel. It would seem that the love that a young Jacob felt for Rachel, and which once was a symbol only of potential, is now the cause of intense grief and has come to symbolize only loss.

And what a poignant final self-portrait of Jacob the reader is given when, in chapter 47—after it has been revealed that Joseph is not only safe but has prospered to the extent that he is now the king of Egypt's right-hand man, and Jacob himself has lived to the ripe old age of 130—Pharaoh asks him, "How many are the years of your life?" Jacob's answer: "few and hard have been the years of my life." His self-assessment is brief and unrelentingly bitter. It is hard to imagine that the heel-grasping baby and the self-assured young man have come to this, but it is a witness to the resolute realism of biblical characterization that they have. The weight of Jacob's life has crushed him.

David is, in some ways, very much like Jacob in that we see him go from a young man full of self-confidence and successful in everything he tries, to a middle-aged man wielding personal and political power, to a bitter old man. But David's story is also very different from Jacob's most especially because of its intense political aspect. (David ruled as king over Israel and Judah for roughly forty years.) The setting for Jacob's power and successes is almost entirely the realm of the personal and the familial. Much of David's story is set in that realm as well (for example, the troubles with his children, beginning with the rape of David's daughter Tamar by his son Amnon in 2 Sam. 13), but it also opens out into the wider realm of the social and the political.

Thus, whereas Jacob's first great successes involved besting his brother Esau and his uncle Laban (the former with the invaluable help of his mother, Rebekah), David's first great success is the very public defeat of Goliath (1 Sam. 17). King Saul, as Israel's protector, should have been the one to defeat Goliath, and his handing of that task over to the young David presages his loss of the throne to David. Though we do not have a birth scene for David, as we do for Jacob, his youth is clearly emphasized when he is introduced into the story, first as the youngest of eight sons in 1 Samuel 16, and then through the reaction of the seasoned warrior Goliath when challenged by David: "When the Philistine looked and saw David, he disdained him, for he was only a youth" (1 Sam. 17:42).

We then see David grow into a mature man and become a wildly successful ruler: "David won a name for himself....And the LORD gave victory to David wherever he went....So David reigned over all Israel; and David administered justice and equity to all his people" (2 Sam. 8:13–15). But of course the story goes on to trace not only David's successes but also his failures (both moral and political), including his sexual taking of Bathsheba and subsequent murder of her husband Uriah, the briefly successful rebellion of his son Absalom, the rape of Tamar, and the rebellion of Sheba. The end of David's life story comes in 1 and 2 Kings: "King David was old and advanced in years; and although they covered him with clothes, he could not get warm" (1 Kgs 1).

Then, on his deathbed in 1 Kings 2:8–9, David instructs his son Solomon to murder the minor character Shimei, who made the mistake of publicly calling David a usurper and "a man of blood" some fifteen chapters and many years earlier in the story. David himself had pledged not to kill Shimei, no doubt for political reasons, but he has not forgotten the slight, and he trusts that his equally ruthless son will settle this old score.

The golden boy David, then, comes to his end as a cold and cynical old man, whose last thought is to avenge a petty slight from years before. No reader could have predicted this end, but when it comes, after we have followed David and seen his faults magnified and his virtues shriveled, it fits the story so well that it seems to have been inevitable. One ought to go back and read through the story, and keep track of David's development as a character. Where is it that things could have gone in another direction? Are there indications earlier in the story that David's end will bitter? And knowing how the story ends, do you now see other ways of filling in David's unstated motivations and his inner life? These are the sorts of literary and moral questions that become possible, and that make for a richer reading experience, by the innovation represented by the long form of prose Hebrew narrative.

The ancient Hebrew short story

While pioneering the long, prose narrative form, the ancient biblical authors also proved skilled at adapting prose narrative to a short form, in essence to a "short story." Our two surviving examples—there may well have been many more circulating in ancient Israel—are the books of Ruth and Esther. In these books we see many of the same elements from extended Hebrew narrative, including most especially the ambiguity and potential complexity of character motivation; what is missing of course is the ability to trace out character and plot development over the course of a lifetime or of several generations. Compensating for that lack is the sort of concentrating effect we find when the plot is condensed to short-story length, resulting in a sharply defined presentation of problem and resolution, the classic way of articulating plot.

The book of Ruth comprises just four short chapters—a couple of pages in most Bibles—and features three main characters: Ruth, her mother-in-law Naomi, and the wealthy landowner Boaz. Although often characterized by interpreters as if they were simple models of fealty, moral rectitude, and piety, these three characters, though existing on the page only briefly, exhibit the same sort of layered complexity we have come to expect from biblical narrative.

Naomi, for example, is nearly always taken to be an example of loving, motherly concern. But if that is the case, why does she allow Ruth to go off into the fields to glean at the beginning of chapter 2 without so much as a word of warning (again, that the situation is potentially dangerous is shown by Boaz's advice to Ruth in 2:9 and his warning to the young male workers in 2:15), and then exhibit an exaggerated motherly care at the end of the chapter, after seeing the interest that Boaz has shown in Ruth? And is it possible that her strenuous attempts to dissuade Ruth and Orpah from returning with her from Moab resulted from a desire not to be burdened with two Moabite women (and two more mouths to feed) in Judah? Does she even imagine that these Moabite women might well be the source of some killing curse, since both her sons died after marrying them (as for example Judah admits to thinking about Tamar in Gen. 38)? The fact is that we just do not know what Naomi is thinking about these or other issues; but our reaction to Naomi and to the developing plot depends on filling these gaps in our knowledge.

So also with Boaz, there is real ambiguity in his approach to Ruth in chapter 2, when he first spies her in his field. Clearly, he displays a keen interest in her, but what is the source and nature of that interest? Is it familial and altruistic, as he implies in his statement in 2:11–12? Or is it sexual or romantic, as the exchange with his foreman (with its emphasis on her Moabite identity) earlier in the chapter might imply? Or are we even to imagine that Boaz himself is not entirely aware of his motivations—after all, at what point does one "realize" that one is interested in another romantically? And of course such interest does not preclude other interests and motivations. And in chapter 3, what is Boaz thinking when he awakes—half-drunk and half-clothed—in the middle of the night, with a woman at his feet? The awkward, rambling syntax of his response to Ruth in 3:10–13 (which seems to mirror the awkward, rambling syntax of Joseph's response to Potiphar's wife as he tries to escape her unwanted sexual advances in Gen. 39) shows us that he is flustered, but we are not told the source and nature of his unease. It is entirely possible, even likely, that he himself is unaware of just what has transpired with this woman— whom he does not recognize at first—and what sort of trouble he might have gotten himself (and her) into. As we wonder what Boaz might be thinking here, we are apt to wonder too about his motivations for "acquiring Ruth the Moabite" (4:10) as wife.

The scene in private at the threshing floor in chapter 3 is in many ways the climactic scene of the book, setting up the final, public resolution of the plot that follows in chapter 4. So it is particularly striking that the scene turns not only on the unstated knowledge and motivations of Boaz but also, and especially, on those of Ruth. There is, in the first place, the question of what exactly Ruth intends to be doing in the scene. When she says to Boaz, "spread your cloak over your servant, for you are next-of-kin" (3:9), is she making an offer of betrothal, as many commentators argue, or is she making an offer of her sexual favors, as a few others have suggested?

And beyond the question of what Ruth is doing, there is question of why she is doing it. Does she actually care for Boaz; does she desire him for herself? (The book is often read in this romantic light.) Does she desire to have a child and take Boaz for a likely father? Or is she acting primarily on behalf of Naomi, in order to give Naomi the heir she needs to secure her legal rights in Judah? Or is it all a strategy for keeping together herself and Naomi, as perhaps suggested by the linking of levirate with next-of-kin duties, since the former apply more to Ruth and the latter to Naomi? The narrator refuses to tell us the answers to any of these questions, although we must surely wonder about them; and the way we as readers choose to answer them determines in no small way how we understand the plot movement and resolution and, to a certain extent, "the meaning" of the book.

The book of Esther, too, exploits the ambiguities of character motivation in striking ways. One freighted example is the question of why the Persian king Ahasueras decides to have Haman executed. Haman has declared himself the enemy of the Jews and has, based on trumped charges, gotten the king to agree to annihilate them. Esther, herself a Jew who has hidden her ethnic identity and become Ahasueras's queen, reveals her Jewishness at a climactic moment in chapter 7, in the presence of both Haman and King Ahasueras. The king storms out in confusion, and Haman throws himself at Esther, apparently to beg for mercy. When the king returns and sees Haman and Esther, he declares his death sentence. It remains unclear whether it is Haman's assault on Esther's Jewishness or a perceived sexual assault that motivates the king's rage at him. If you read the book through, you may notice that it is intensely concerned with both ethnic and gender identity, and the ways in which such identities are both important and in many ways unstable. It is certainly no accident that at the climactic moment of the plot, both of these themes are brought together into the foreground in such a way that we cannot know for sure which is finally more important. The point being, of course, that both are, but that individual readers must negotiate for themselves whether they think one or the other is foremost in Ahasueras's mind at this point and why that might be.

This sort of climactic plot moment is rare in the longer biblical narratives, which develop more slowly and will sometimes even seem episodic. In the longer narratives one might identify any number of places where a plot-changing event occurs, or where a particularly momentous decision is made by a character, but rarely will such a dramatic resolution take place, since the reader's interest must be sustained over the long haul of the narrative. But with short narratives such as Esther and Ruth, the concentrated form of the plot allows for a more intense manifestation of the central conflict and its resolution. The book of Esther achieves this climax by bringing together the twin themes of gender and ethnic identity just at the moment that the governing conflict of the plot—How will Haman's genocidal decree against the Jews be nullified?—comes to a head and is resolved by the (ironic) death sentence against Haman himself.

The book of Ruth has an equally compact and neatly articulated plot, although without such a classic protagonist/antagonist relationship. The central problem that the plot in Ruth works out is the question of how Ruth and Naomi will survive now that their legal rights and means of support have disappeared with the death of all the men in the family (Naomi's husband, Elimelech, and her two sons, one of whom was Ruth's husband; see 1:1–5). The death and destitution that characterize Naomi's family finds symbolic counterpart in the famine that forces the family to leave their hometown of Bethlehem at the start of the book (ironically, in Hebrew the name Bethlehem literally means "house of bread," where now of course there is no bread to be found). After the death of her husband and sons, Naomi hears that the famine has broken and she returns, with Ruth following, to Bethlehem. The women's immediate need for food is met by Ruth's gleaning in the field of Boaz (ch. 2), but the problem of their long-term security and restored legal rights remains at the forefront.

The plot of the book comes to a head in chapter 3. This scene offers the solution to the problem of survival faced by Naomi and Ruth, by attaching them to Boaz, and chapter 4 of the book offers a classic *dénouement*, or "unraveling" of the remaining plot threads. But one of the things that makes the neatness of the plot more complex and interesting is that alongside the primary issue of the survival of Naomi and Ruth, there exists the secondary and in many ways more interesting issue: Will Ruth and Naomi be able to stay together? This issue is foregrounded by Ruth's compelling speech in 1:16–17, where she pledges absolute loyalty to Naomi. Also driving the plot, then, is the problem of how Ruth can fulfill this vow of solidarity. By making Boaz an offer that includes both marriage to her and the legal redemption of the land belonging to Naomi, Ruth (and thus the plot of the book) has tied together the women's survival with their solidarity and has ensured both.

Chapter 3
Reading biblical poetry

Robert Frost once proclaimed, only somewhat tongue in cheek, that poetry is "that which is lost in translation." The point being that so much of what constitutes poetry can be found in what is sometimes referred to as the "musicality" of its language: the sounds, the rhythms, the structure of its syntax, the way particular words echo other meanings. It is true that nearly all of these aspects of poetry are lost in translation and, unless one is reading biblical poetry in Hebrew, one must always keep in mind that there is much in terms of poetic art that cannot be carried over into another language. But of course, not *all* is lost, for there are other aspects that do carry over; and an awareness of those aspects can make the reading of biblical poetry a richer and more productively complex experience.

One of the great, recurrent themes of poetry across cultures and historical periods is love. And so it seems appropriate to begin this discussion of biblical poetry with some lines from the Song of Songs (also known as the Song of Solomon), the sole surviving example of erotic poetry from ancient Israel. Some people are surprised to learn that erotic poetry even exists in the Bible, though perhaps we ought not to be, since the ancient Hebrews were no more immune to the power of *erōs* than anyone else and since the Bible is not only a collection of

so-called religious texts and but also an anthology of literary
achievement.

Near the end of the Song of Songs, after seven chapters in which
an alternating male and female voice express their desire for one
another in lush, metaphorical language, the reader comes upon a
rare second-order reflection on the nature of love, rather than the
first-person declarations and descriptions encountered to this
point in the book. Here is what the lines look like in printed
Hebrew script:

שימני כחותם על־לבך

כחותם על־זרועך

כי־עזה כמות אהבה

קשה כשאול קנאה

רשפיה רשפי אש

שלהבתיה

Without knowing the Hebrew alphabet, one cannot make heads
or tails of this. But if we transliterate the lines—rewriting them in
a basic phonetic representation—you can read them out loud and
hear, roughly, how they sound in the original language:

simeni kakhotam al libbeka

kakhotam al zero'eka

ki azzah kammavet 'ahavah

qashah kesheol qin'ah

reshapheyha rishpey esh

shalhevetyah

A very literal, word for word translation of these lines (with single
Hebrew words represented by hyphenated clauses, and missing
but implied verbs in parentheses) might go like this:

Set-me as-a-seal upon your-heart,

as-a-seal upon your-arm;

for strong as-death (is) love,
hard as-the-grave (is) jealousy.
its-sparks (are) sparks-of fire,
a-raging-flame.

And here now is a more standard English translation of these lines from the widely used New Revised Standard Version (NRSV) of the Bible, which smooths out the syntax and follows the common practice of representing the second line of a couplet with indentation:

Set me as a seal upon your heart,
 as a seal upon your arm;
for love is strong as death,
 passion fierce as the grave.
Its flashes are flashes of fire,
 a raging flame. (Song 8:6)

Even if a reader does not know Hebrew, and thus cannot take any meaning from the transliterated lines, he or she can begin to see how the lines work as poetry and how something is lost in the English version. In particular, there is the strong sounding of the /k/ sound in the first four lines: "kakhotam . . . kakhotam . . . ki azzah kamavet . . . qashah kesheol qin'ah." The relation of sound to meaning is always a tricky one, but nevertheless I am tempted to say that the hardness of that alliterated /k/ is meant to reflect the hardness of passion ("hard" being the more literal rendering of the Hebrew word *qashah*, or "fierce" in the NRSV). And then there are the repeated /r/s and /sh/s in the final two lines, which soften the hardness of the /k/, only to replace it with the threat of a raging flame.

The Hebrew has a nice aural rhythm to it, but the NRSV's English version is not bad either in that respect, falling into a loose iambic meter. And if the alliterated /k/s and /r/s and /sh/s are lost, the translators have nevertheless alliterated rather nicely on the /s/s and /f/s. One might notice that five of the six Hebrew lines rhyme with each other, while the English has only the near-rhyme of "heart" with "arm." In fact, rhyme in biblical poetry is really pretty rare, its occurrence here calling attention to itself and to these lines. So something is perhaps lost by not having the rhyme in English.

There is also noticeable loss at the level of diction, or word choice, since several of the Hebrew words call up mythical or theological associations in a way that the English equivalents do not. For example, the reference to "death" (Hebrew: *mavet*) in line 3 is a clear allusion to the Canaanite god Mot (= "Death"), the reference to "sparks" (here the plural form of the Hebrew *reshef*) alludes to the Canaanite god Reshef (= "Firebolt"), and the final word *shalhevetyah*, translated by the NRSV as "a raging flame," explicitly contains a part of the divine name Yahweh, the proper name of Israel's god. The *-yah* attached to the end of the word *shalhevet* ("fire") functions here as a grammatical intensifier, thus justifying the NRSV's "*raging* flame"; but an ancient reader of the poem in Hebrew would surely have caught the particle of divinity that this neologism incorporates, especially in light of the references to the other divinities Mot and Reshef. Of course a modern reader can pick up these allusions from a scholarly commentary, but that's not quite the same experience as hearing the double meaning simultaneously, as it adheres in the language itself. And while some translators have tried to incorporate that double meaning in the translation—Marcia Falk has "a fierce and holy blaze" and the New Jerusalem Bible has "a flame of Yahweh himself"—attempts to do so come off as more obviously theological than does the Hebrew.

No doubt there is even more that is lost in reading these lines in English translation, but what can we say about what is *not* lost? What is it that marks these lines as poetry and allows the reader to interpret them "as poetry and not another thing" (to recall Eliot)? There are several such elements to be identified in these lines from the Song of Songs, elements shared by poetry throughout the

Hebrew Bible, and paying attention to them in these lines and beyond will provide an overall picture of how Hebrew biblical poetry works.

Lineation

The presence of lines is the most basic element in most definitions of poetry. Poetry is "verse," lined out on the page (or to the ear), as opposed to "prose," where line length is variable and depends only on the space available. Biblical verse most often, by far, takes the form of couplets or triplets, two or three lines bound to each other more strongly than they are to other lines within the same poem, although it does seem that occasionally there occurs a freestanding line not matched with another. Since Robert Lowth's groundbreaking revaluing of ancient Hebrew poetry in the eighteenth century, when he used the Latin phrase *parallelismus membrorum* to refer to the "parallelism of lines," the relationship between lines in a couplet or triplet has most often been thought of in terms of "parallelism," where one or more aspects of the first line are paralleled in the second or third line. The parallelism may be grammatical, syntactical, phonological ("sounds"), or semantic, though it is usually the latter, a parallelism of "meaning," that comes over in translation.

We can clearly see this parallelism between lines in, for example, the first couplet from my very literal translation of the Song of Songs 8:6:

> Set-me   as-a-seal   upon your-heart,
> [set-me]   as-a-seal   upon your-arm.

Although the verb is dropped in the second line, it is present by implication, and all the other elements are grammatically and syntactically matched in the two lines. And as the transliterated lines show, there is a strong phonological match between the lines, with both vowel and consonant sounds repeated and even a final rhyme (which is a form of parallelism). So too with the second couplet from Song of Songs 8:6, where there exists an even stronger correlation, with every syntactical element in the first line, after the opening particle "for," having a match in the second line, and with both the alliteration of the /k/ sound and the final rhyme providing phonological parallels.

The third couplet (lines 5 and 6), however, indicates the ways in which the relationship between lines can go beyond a straightforwardly parallel structure. Although clearly connected by the image of flame, the lines display little of the syntactical or phonological parallelism present in the other couplets. But the semantic relationship between the line does serve as an example of a characteristic phenomenon found throughout biblical Hebrew poetry, namely, a dynamic relationship in which the second line moves beyond the first in significant ways. In this case, the "sparks" and "fire" of the first line become the "raging flame" of the second line.

Even when the relationship between lines looks to be semantically parallel at first glance, there is often a subtle dynamism in which the second line pushes forward the language or imagery in the first by making it more concrete, more focused or specific, more intense, or more emotionally heightened. Thus, even within the strict parallelism of the second couplet, we may recognize that *jealousy* is a more specific emotion associated with *love*; *harsh* heightens and intensifies the connotation of *strong*; and *the grave* serves as a concrete symbol of *death*. The first couplet offers an interesting test case, in that many readers will no doubt feel that when it comes to love a seal "on the heart" is more intense than a seal "on the arm"; it is likely that the dynamic we see here then is the movement from abstract ("heart" as inner life) to concrete ("arm"), with a concomitant intensification from the private feeling of love to public declaration.

While there are some couplets that exhibit a truly synonymous parallelism, with no discernible development from one line to the next, such a static relationship is relatively rare; part of both the task and the fun of reading biblical poetry is pausing to think about the particular variety of parallelism in any given couplet (or triplet). Here is a typical fully parallel couplet (2 Sam. 22:30), from a long poem spoken by King David near the end of his life, in which he attributes his military successes to God:

| For | with you | I charge | a barrier, |
| | with my God | I vault | a wall. |

Even with such close parallelism (shown in my spacing of the lines) we still find a development of specification and intensification, with a "wall" being a more specific example of the general category of barrier and with "vault" being a stronger verb and a stronger claim than charge. We also see a typical chronological movement: first one charges the barrier, and then one vaults the wall. Moreover, the heightened claim of the second line may be thought of as, "Well, charging in battle is one thing, the question is what happens when you get to the barrier/wall." One could turn around and retreat for example, or one could sit in siege outside the wall waiting for something to happen, or one could get shot in the throat by an arrow. But David's claim here is, "Not only did I charge, but with God's help I vaulted the wall and was thus victorious." This parallel structure of "not only... but also..." is one way of characterizing the sort of heightening or adding-on that occurs repeatedly in second couplet lines.

A characteristic three-line sequence, or triplet, occurs in v. 9 of the same poem by David, in a poetic vision of God as divine warrior:

Smoke went up from his nostrils,
and fire from his mouth consumed,
coals glowed around him. (2 Sam. 22:9)

Binding the three lines is the triad "smoke / fire / coals." Binding further the first two lines is the word-pair "nostrils / mouth."

Without the third line we would have here a fairly standard couplet, with "smoke" intensifying to the more destructive "fire" and the verb "went up" intensifying to "consumed." The addition of the third line continues the fire imagery and the chronological sequence (first the smoke came out, then the fire consumed, then the coals glowed) but takes the emphasis off the divine body (there is no match for nostrils or mouth) and onto the destruction that has been wreaked. God stokes God's anger in the first line, then blasts with destructive fire in the second, which reduces everything around to glowing coals in the third.

Elements of biblical poetic style

Beyond the question of line articulation, however, the cluster of other features that typify biblical verse has mostly been overlooked. But one can get a much richer sense of the distinctive workings of biblical poetic style by recognizing these features—features that can be seen more clearly when compared with the workings of biblical prose narrative.

By casting their stories in the form of prose, ancient Hebrew authors pioneered a writerly form of narrative that did not depend on the rhythms of oral poetry and that allowed for the development of a genuine third-person narrator, whose voice could be distinguished from the direct discourse attributed to characters within the narrative. It also allowed for a depth-of-consciousness and an opaqueness in its literary characters rarely found in ancient narrative: readers are seldom told what characters are thinking or feeling at any given moment, even though it is often vitally important to characterization and to plot development. We have seen that this lack of access to inner lives is part of the laconic style of biblical narrative, where so much is left unexpressed and where neither people nor objects are much described.

Hebrew poetry, however, works very differently than Hebrew narrative. In the first place there are the formal differences that mark verse: not only lineation but also a sort of collapsed syntax that tends to drop particles and pronouns in order to achieve the compression of the line. Such compression, or concision, is commonly associated with poetry generally and in many languages, and is often thought responsible for the semantically saturated nature of poetic discourse, the way that poetry achieves a maximum of meaning with a minimum of words. Scholars have noticed, for example, that three Hebrew particles in particular—the relative pronoun *'asher* ("which" or "who") the definite direct object marker *'et* (which is untranslatable), and the definite article *ha-* ("the")—are quite commonly found in prose but much less so in poetry, to the extent that these are sometimes termed "prose particles" and used as a primary distinguishing criterion for poetry. The data, collected and presented by Andersen-Forbes and by Freedman, is indeed striking, showing that statistically these particles count for less than 5 percent of the words in biblical books that appear to be poetry and for more than 15 percent in the more obviously prose books. And the books of the prophets, which mix poetry and prose, tend to fall right in between these percentages.

This markedly concise syntax, then, can be taken as a formal indicator of poetry—"formal" in the sense of inhering in the form of the literature, and not dependent on any special theme or content. But it is probably best to consider the issue of so-called prose particles within the context of a larger impulse toward conciseness in Hebrew poetry, the absence of particles representing one strategy for realizing the typically short poetic line. We need not spend any more time here on the technicalities of syntactical structure or particle percentages, since these elements are available only when reading the Hebrew; nonetheless, they are important because they help translators establish the lines, which are essential for distinguishing verse from prose. And even in translation we are likely to notice the relative brevity of clauses and lines in comparison with prose biblical texts.

Biblical poetry is also, to borrow Terry Eagleton's vague but appropriate characterization of poetry in general, much more "verbally inventive" than biblical prose narrative. The terse, straightforward style of biblical narrative means that it tends to avoid elevated diction or figurative language. Indeed, one is hard pressed to find biblical narrators using even the most basic of metaphors, and when metaphorical language does appear in narrative it is nearly always placed in the voice of characters. This stylistic convention contributes to the nascent realism that ancient Hebrew authors developed as they exploited the new technology of writing to cultivate this new style of narrative. Part of that realism, too, would seem to be an impulse toward avoiding a simple and straightforward portrayal of divine activity in history, taking the form not only of an avoidance of mythological stories of gods and monsters but also of an often paradoxical articulation of divine agency being bound up and even dependent on human agency.

Biblical poetry, by contrast, displays no such commitment to realism, brimming with a wide range of figurative language and alluding more freely to mythological contexts and to God's concrete intervention in history. Because this aspect of poetic style inheres in the content and meaning of the words, rather than the grammar or syntax, it tends to be available to readers in translation. For example, in Song of Songs 8:6 we saw the speaker metaphorically imagine herself as a seal for the arm or heart of her beloved, and love was compared figuratively both to death and to fire. Moreover, those comparisons invoked mythological associations with the gods Mot and Reshef in a fairly explicit way.

Some of the figurative language found in biblical poetry can be quite conventional or familiar sounding. The troubled fate of the psalmist is, often as not, imagined metaphorically in terms of "the pit" that threatens to swallow or "the flood" that threatens to overwhelm, and God is regularly imagined as a "rock," a "fortress," or a "shield." The conventional nature of metaphor in the psalms is not surprising, and should not be taken as a failure of imagination on the part of the poets, since the psalms were written to be used communally in a liturgical context (and are still widely used in such contexts, both Jewish and Christian), where startling images and complex figures of thought might hinder communal recitation. It is also the case that endless generations of private readers have found solace or inspiration in the conventional language of the psalms. In each of these cases, the communal and the private devotional, the relatively unadventurous and nonspecific nature of figurative language has allowed a wide variety of readers to adopt for themselves the voice of the psalmist. If continued reuse and relevance is any guide, then the mostly anonymous poets behind the psalms may be judged among the most successful poets of all time.

For more inventive uses of figurative language and imagery, we may look to the book of Job. Consider, for example, Job's curse in chapter 3 of that book. In his imaginative blotting out of the day of his birth, the suffering Job both personifies and eroticizes it, representing the night as longing for the day which, in his counterfactual curse, never arrives:

> Let the stars of its dawn be dark;
>> let it long for light in vain,
>>> and never behold the eyelids of morning. (3:9)

The metaphor works nicely for a couple of reasons. One is that it expresses the basic theme of the poem: Job's longing for the release that comes with death, figured here as the nonexistence that would result from the blotting out of the day of his birth. Job's longing seems to provide the central metaphor for the lines, but it is transformed into erotic longing in the process and becomes attached, as erotic longing properly ought to be, to the night rather than to the day. Paradoxically then, Job longs for the "night" of nonexistence even as the personified night longs for the very day that Job hopes to annihilate. The futility of the night's longing for a day that never arrives suggests as well the futility of Job's curse; he cannot, the poetry implicitly acknowledges, go back and erase the day in question. And as if to illustrate the ways in which the nuances of poetic figuration outstrip the necessities of theme, the poet does not just say that night will never meet morning but that it will never "behold the *eyelids* of morning." The specificity of "eyelids" extends the eroticism of the poem (furtive glances being a first sign of erotic desire), but it also embodies another metaphor for dawn, in which the sun coming up on the horizon is figured as the opening of an eye.

The poet also has Job, a few chapters later in the book, imagine God's enmity toward him in terms of the ancient grudge between God-as-creator and the chaotic force of the personified Sea, alluding explicitly to Canaanite mythology, where "Sea" is the meaning of the god Yamm's name (in Hebrew *yam*):

> Am I the Sea, or the Dragon,
>> that you set a guard over me? (7:12; cf. 3:8; 26:12)

Answering Job, thirty chapters later in the book, the poet has God return to this image, but redefines and repersonifies the chaotic Sea not as an enemy combatant but as an infant to be nurtured:

> Who is it that contained the Sea
>> as it emerged bursting from the womb?—
> when I clothed it in clouds,
>> and swaddled it with darkness. (38:8–9)

This poetic reimagining carries with it theological and cosmological implications, and here we can see more of the Job poet's inventiveness. As a force of chaos and a threat to the good order of the world, the personified Sea is elsewhere imagined as an enemy of the creator God. Refiguring this great, threatening monster as a little baby is quite a poetic move, though not as reassuring as it might seem, since it is a baby that God is portrayed as caring for and nurturing. The creator God, who ought to represent orderliness and reliability, is thus associated with the forces of chaos and indeed is portrayed as securing a place for those forces in the cosmos rather than attempting to eradicate them.

This initial image of God-sponsored chaos is consonant with the rest of the god-speeches of the book of Job (in 38:1–41:34), which are prime material for both delicate and soaring use of figurative language, and which culminate in extensive description of the chaos monsters Behemoth and Leviathan, the latter a well-known mythological figure and the former perhaps invented by the poet to serve as the immovable weight in contrast to Leviathan's unstoppable force. Leviathan here (ch. 41) is no longer the infant Sea but now a full-fledged monster: "When it raises itself up the gods are afraid; / at the crashing they are beside themselves" (41:25). And yet, still the poet imagines this Leviathan not as an enemy of God but rather as a creature worthy of God's admiration: "I will not keep silence concerning its limbs, / or its mighty strength, or its splendid frame" (41:12). In fact, although many translations cover this over, God at one point slips into the first person in describing Leviathan: "No one is so fierce as to dare to stir it up. / Who can stand before me?" (41:10). Is God describing the terror of Leviathan or the terror of the divine self? In either case, it is clear that the poet associates God with Leviathan and thus, surprisingly, claims a place for the chaotic within God's creation.

The Song of Songs represents a very different poetic idiom than the book of Job but is perhaps its equal as a high point of ancient Hebrew verse. Erotic poetry set in the alternating voices of two young, unmarried lovers, the Song of Songs prefers a lush, bodily-based array of metaphors. For example, the male voice proclaims:

> Your breasts are like two fawns,
>> twins of a gazelle,
>>> that feed among the lilies. (4:5)

Or this, from the female voice:

> Like an apple tree found in the forest
> > is my beloved among the youths;
> I delight to sit in his shade,
> > and his fruit is sweet to my taste. (2:3)

Some of the figurative language in the Song of Songs would appear to function as double entendres, but certainly not all have a straightforwardly translatable sexual content. Indeed, the anonymous poet (or poets) behind the Song of Songs seems to revel in the production of metaphors and similes out of sheer literary creativity. As Robert Alter puts it, "in the Song of Songs the process of figuration is frequently 'foregrounded,'" with the poetry calling attention to "the artifice of metaphorical representation." In reading the Song of Songs then, one should look not only for how the many metaphors and similes serve to represent erotic desire, but also how they generate meaning in excess of what the context requires.

One could multiply many times over these few instances of figurative language from biblical poetry, filling countless pages with examples of metaphor, simile, personification, apostrophe, prosopopeia, etc. And one could also cite many more examples in which ancient Hebrew poets cited or alluded to or evoked mythological stories and characters, or in which they imagined concrete divine action in the world. What is striking is how very few pages one could fill with similar examples from prose narrative.

The uses of biblical poetry

If line structure and other formal markers are enough to establish the presence and basic style of verse in the Bible, they still do not tell us much about its use or function. Again, a comparison with biblical prose is instructive, since one of the most striking features of biblical poetry is that it is relentlessly non-narrative. Once ancient Hebrew culture had developed the flexible prose form that gets used for recounting stories, both long (e.g., Gen. 1 and 2 Sam.) and short (e.g., the books of Ruth and Esther), it seems that verse was reserved for more specialized, highly rhetorical uses.

For example, the prophets are most often represented as casting their messages in poetic form, even while narratives about the prophets are in prose. Note the parallelism and figurative language in, for example, Amos's well-known *cri de coeur*,

> Let justice roll down like the waters,
> > and righteousness like a mighty stream. (Am 5:24)

This familiar parallel structure is combined with hyperbole and a striking visual imagination (elements both quite rare in biblical narrative, though common in ancient epic poetry traditions) in the prophet Isaiah's utopian vision of the future:

> The wolf shall live with the lamb,
> > and the leopard shall lie down with the kid. (Isa. 11:6)

This utopian vision, however, is far more positive than the prophets tend to be, and typically we find prophetic poetry using the additive nature of poetic parallelism to drive home their critique of social and religious failings. Amos's scathing judgment on exploitative greed takes this classic parallelistic form:

> They sell the righteous for silver,
> > and the needy for a pair of sandals–
> they who trample the head of the poor into the dust of the earth,
> > and push the afflicted out of the way. (Am 2:7)

The result of this greed? According to Amos, God threatens divine retribution, again in a classic poetic form that utilizes not only repetition but strategic advancement (first the fire comes, then it destroys) and a specifying focus (from the larger territory of Judah to the cityscape of Jerusalem):

> So I will send a fire on Judah,
>> and it shall devour the strongholds of Jerusalem. (Am 2:5)

As with the Job poet, prophets too will make use of mythological imagery, especially the monsters, which they sometimes use as political metaphors, as for example in Isaiah 51:9 where God's violent destruction of the chaos monsters Rahab and the dragon presage the fall of the Babylonian empire, or in Ezekiel 29:3-6 and 32:2-6 where the king of Egypt is imagined as a "dragon in the seas" (32:2) who will be butchered by God ("I will strew your flesh on the mountains, / and fill the valleys with your carcass" [32:5]). Elsewhere in the prophets, the mythological monsters seem to represent a more generalized, cosmic chaos, a recognition that the world is not right and a hope that one day—the final day—God will finally defeat the forces of chaos:

> On that day the Lord will punish
>> with his cruel and great and strong sword
> Leviathan the fleeing serpent,
>> Leviathan the twisting serpent,
>>> he will kill the dragon in the sea. (Isa. 27:1)

Verse also seems to have been the preferred form in ancient Hebrew, as in so many languages, for the aphorism—the pithy and often didactic observation on the nature of the world—which, like poetry more generally, aims to maximize the meaning of a few carefully chosen words. The book of Proverbs is filled with such aphorisms in verse form. For example:

> A soft answer turns away wrath,
>> but a harsh word stirs up anger. (Prov. 15:1)

> Better is a dinner of vegetables where love is,
>> than a fatted ox and hatred with it. (15:17)

Like the cold of snow in the time of harvest
    are faithful messengers to those who send them;
        they refresh the spirit of their masters. (25:13)

As a door turns on its hinges,
    so does a lazy person in bed. (26:14)

These translations from the NRSV, as with virtually all translations, lose much of the compactness of the Hebrew, where any given poetic line rarely contains more than four words. Nevertheless, we see in these and other proverbial sayings from the Bible all the basic elements of Hebrew poetry, including parallelism, figurative language, and even in English an observable conciseness.

For all the vividness and wit, the aphorisms in the book of Proverbs are essentially conservative in their vision of a knowable, morally ordered world. For more skeptical examples, however, one can turn to the book of Ecclesiastes, as in

All streams run to the sea,
    but the sea is never filled...
The eye is not satisfied with seeing,
    nor the ear filled with hearing. (Eccl 1:7–8)

Or,

With much wisdom comes much grief;
    to increase knowledge is to increase sorrow. (1:18)

The author of Ecclesiastes seems to come from the same intellectual circles as the authors of Proverbs and uses the same tools of verse, but he uses poetry to generate a world-weary cynicism rather to express a confident authority.

One of the most interesting uses of biblical verse is as an early form of what will later go by name of "lyric poetry": that intensely subjective, nonnarrative and nondramatic form that has dominated modern English and European poetry since the eighteenth century. The category of lyric foregrounds two final characteristics of biblical poetry, both of which further distinguish it from biblical prose narrative.

First, biblical poetry is invariably presented as direct discourse, the first-person voice of a speaking subject (a precursor of the modern "lyric I"). Again, ancient Hebrew narrative separates the third-person narrator from the dialogue spoken by characters, which is grammatically marked (by expressive forms and deictics) as direct discourse, whereas the narrator's voice is not. (The indispensable scholarly work here is Robert Kawashima's book *Biblical Narrative and the Death of the Rhapsode*.)

Biblical poetry is also marked in this way; it is, in other words, always presented as if it were dialogue. So, for example, the biblical narrator seems never to be represented as speaking in poetry, but characters quite often are, as in long poems like the deathbed blessing of Jacob, the Song of the Sea, the Song of Moses, the Song of Deborah, David's lament over Jonathan and Saul, and so forth. These extended poems have long been recognized, but we now also know that characters will break into poetry on a smaller scale as well, such as the two poems put into the mouths of Naomi and Ruth in chapter 1 of the book of Ruth or, on an even smaller scale, the two lines uttered by Jacob upon seeing the bloodied garment of Joseph, which as Alter has noted in his translation of Genesis take the form of a classically articulated poetic couplet: "a vicious beast has devoured him, / torn, torn is Joseph" (*hayya ra'ah akhalatehu / tarof toraf yosef*). This criterion of direct discourse means, however, that Alter is probably wrong to identify Genesis 1:27 as verse ("And God created the human in his image, / in the image of God he created him, / male and female he created them"), since it is presented as the voice of the narrator. This judgment is confirmed by the presence in the verse of the verb-form of choice for prose narration (the *vav*-consecutive imperfect" form, for those who know Hebrew) and by four instances of "prose particles" in only twelve words.

The second way that biblical poetry distinguishes itself from narrative is in its willingness to give access to the inner lives of its speakers. Nearly every standard handbook of literary terms associates the lyric mode with the expression of feeling "in a personal and subjective fashion," to quote a particularly influential one. And if biblical narrative trades in opaqueness of characterization, biblical poetry fairly revels in the exposure of subjectivity. When biblical authors wanted to convey feeling or thought, they resorted to verse form. Obvious examples of this formal preference include poetic books like the Psalms and the Song of Songs, where the expression of passion, whether despairing or joyful, is common.

But we also find that the poetic insets in narrative contexts often serve to express or intensify emotion (as for example Jacob's reaction to the bloodied robe of Joseph) or to otherwise grant the reader access to the inner lives of characters. This practice by biblical authors of dropping poems into prose narratives is worth considering in more detail, as it helps to further delineate the distinctive elements of ancient Hebrew verse and prose literature, respectively, even as it shows how they could be deliberately brought together as complementary forms in a larger literary work. And this will be our next topic.

Chapter 4
Narrative and poetry working together

Ancient Hebrew literary culture comprises two primary and distinct modes of expression: narrative and poetry. The result is a sort of literary division of labor, each with its own forms and techniques and tools, as well as its own functions and subgenres. Biblical narrative takes the form of prose, works out the tensions of plot and character, trades in ambiguity and unstated motivation, and evinces a stripped-down style that avoids fancy words and figurative language. Biblical poetry takes the form of lined-out verse, is fundamentally nonnarrative in nature (with no real plot or characters), and revels in the play of language, the generating of metaphor, and the vivid expression of thought and feeling. Although these distinctions have been little recognized by either scholars or, apparently, casual readers of the Bible, they are for the most part consistently present in the literature. Confusing the nature and workings of biblical narrative and poetry diminishes the experience of reading them.

And yet, it must be admitted that the Bible itself brings the two forms together on occasion, not in such a way as to confuse them but to maintain and make use of the distinctive literary resources of each. Narrative and poetry do work together sometimes in biblical literature, precisely in order to exploit the possibilities of each. Even though biblical narrative proper never takes the form of verse, verse nevertheless has an important role to play in biblical narrative.

Epic poetry in ancient Israel?

Before considering the function of poetry in biblical narrative, it is worth asking whether extended verse narrative actually existed in ancient Israel. Is it simply the case that the Israelites never produced verse narrative, or is it rather that such narrative existed but did not make it into the canon of the Hebrew Scriptures and thus disappeared from the literary record? Scholars have long debated this question, often phrased, as the title of an important article by Shemaryahu Talmon puts it, as "Did There Exist a National Biblical Epic?"

The term "epic" is borrowed from the Greek (*epos*), and is generally understood to mean long, narrative poems with roots in oral performance, often recounting the acts of gods and of human heroes. Nearly everyone agrees that we do not find genuine epic in the Bible precisely because of the prose form that Hebrew narrative inevitably takes, whereas epic is by most accounts partly defined by its verse form. While it seems entirely possible, and perhaps probable, that there existed some form of epic poetry in ancient Israel, this poetry remains unavailable to us. In order to say anything more about the relationship of poetry to biblical narrative, then, we must move in a different direction, asking what role the essentially nonnarrative poetry that we have might play in relation to biblical narrative. For in fact, poetry shows up not infrequently within biblical narrative, even if it is not the primary formal mode. That is, within the bodies of prose narrative in the Bible one finds many places where the literature shifts into verse form, and it is worth asking what the various authors or editors achieve by bringing poetry into what is an overwhelmingly nonpoetic form.

Poems as markers of structure

Perhaps the first thing to notice about the use of poetry in narrative contexts is that it often seems to mark a particularly prominent structural point in a developing plot, in a biblical book, or in some other canonical unit. For example, two of the most prominent poems in the Torah (the first five books of the Bible) are Jacob's deathbed blessing of his twelve sons in Genesis 49:2–27 and Moses's blessing of the twelve tribes of Israel in Deuteronomy 33:2–29. Both of these long poems function as parade examples of the genre "testamentary blessing," that is, a final blessing by an important character, usually a father or father figure, given before the character dies. Likely these were preexisting compositions that an author or editor worked into their present narrative contexts. Whatever their prehistory, they function now to mark the end of the respective life stories of Jacob and Moses, two especially significant figures for Israel's sense of self-identity, even as the blessing genre, emphasizing as it does the waiting future, opens out to the next stage of the story.

The blessing-poems of Jacob and Moses have, as well, a clear structural significance that goes beyond the immediate context of the life-plots of their respective speakers, since they also mark the endings of the books of which they are a part. In each case there remains a chapter of prose narrative to come (Gen. 50 and Deut. 34, respectively), but the poems prepare for those prose endings by slowing the reader down and by adding a rhetorical gravitas to the proceedings. The book of Deuteronomy is the last book in the Torah, and perhaps because of that we find two poems near the end of the book, reinforcing not only the close of the book but also the close of the larger canonical unit. Thus, just before his testamentary blessing in chapter 33, we find Moses uttering the long poem in 32:1–43, traditionally known as the *ha-azinu* (from its first Hebrew word, "listen") or as "the Song of Moses." This poem functions well to mark the ending of the Torah, focused as it is on the fraught relationship between God and Israel, rooted in the saving actions of God on Israel's behalf (vv. 4–14) but including also the predicted disobedience of Israel (vv. 15–18, 28–33) and abandonment on God's part (vv. 19–27).

This deliberate use of poems to mark noteworthy moments or important structural points in biblical narrative is not limited to endings. The justly famous poem (the "Song of the Sea") in Exodus 15:1–18, for example, seems to function as a marker of Israel's transition from slavery to freedom, a major moment not only in the book of Exodus but in the larger biblical story. A similar, but somewhat more complicated structural employment of poetry can be found in 1 and 2 Samuel, which recount the rise of kingship in Israel, initially in the person of Saul and later, more successfully, with David.

In many ways the books of Samuel exemplify the very best of ancient Hebrew narrative technique: a lengthy, artful, and coherent story, with complicated and conflicted characters who grow and change over the course of their lifetimes and who (unlike most ancient literary characters) are capable of surprising the reader. The story contains plot twists and turns, makes use of subtly deployed keywords and themes, and excels in the artful rendering of dialogue. Like all biblical narrative, the books of Samuel are almost entirely in prose, though in about half a dozen places or so characters are presented as speaking (or singing) in verse form. There a few brief poetic insets, such as Samuel's classic prophetic criticism of Saul in 1 Samuel 15:22–23, the two lines of a victory song attributed to "the women" in 1 Samuel 18:7 (and repeated by the Philistine courtiers in 21:11), and David's brief dirge for Abner in 2 Samuel 3:34. But there are also three long poems, placed strategically at the beginning, middle, and end of the larger narrative. These three poems—the "Song of Hannah" in 1 Samuel 2:1–10, David's lament over Saul and Jonathan in 2 Samuel 1:19–27, and David's psalm of praise in 2 Samuel 22:2–51—not only bookend or frame the narrative but also divide it into two nearly equal sections.

The Song of Hannah marks the beginning of the story by underscoring the birth of Samuel, the prophet who will anoint the first (and then second) king of Israel, and by offering a vision of

Yahwistic justice that is to be embodied by the future king ("The Lord will judge the ends of the earth; / he will give strength to his king, / and exalt the power of his anointed" [1 Sam. 2:10]). One of the driving tensions of the plot of the books of Samuel is that the first chosen and anointed king, Saul, is finally a failure and must be replaced by David. It is precisely this midnarrative tipping-point moment—the moment that Saul has died but David has yet to officially replace him—that is marked by David's dirge in 2 Samuel 1.

The transitional function of the poem is exhibited by the way in which it begins by emphasizing the third-person "pastness" of Saul and Jonathan ("they were swifter than eagles, / they were stronger than lions"), before moving into the first-person present of David ("I am distressed for you, my brother Jonathan"). The third of the long poems, prepares both David and the reader for the end of the story of Israel's first successful king. Spoken in the first person, like the ending of his lament over Saul and Jonathan, David's own achievements are now also rendered in the past ("you exalted me above my enemies, / you delivered me from the violent" [22:49]). Moreover, this long poem (over one hundred lines) is paired with the shorter "last words of David," which immediately begin in 23:1-7. Although there remains considerable debate about the origins and dating of all three of these poems, it seems likely that they were added to the narrative relatively late in order to, among other things, mark the beginning, middle, and end of the final form of the origin-narrative of Israelite kingship.

The weight of poetry

Beyond serving to frame narratives or mark structurally important moments in them, we find inset poems functioning in a few other ways in narrative contexts. Although it appears to be the case that the third-person biblical narrator will never speak in poetry, there are quite a few poems, ranging from just two lines (biblical poetry rarely if ever appears in a narrative context in the form of a single line on its own) to a couple of dozen, attributed to various characters throughout the stories. In the garden of Eden story, for example, we encounter two verse sections: one brief (Gen. 2:23) and one longer (Gen. 3:14–19). In both of these—the first man's response to the creation of the first woman and God's response to the eating of the prohibited fruit, respectively—the poetry functions to add a certain weight, gravitas, or solemnity to the speech of the characters.

Using the formal qualities of verse to add a formality of tone to the speech of characters is one of the most common ways that poetry functions in biblical narrative. In the book of Genesis alone we find some twenty examples of poems functioning this way, from God's vow in 8:22 never to bring again a worldwide flood, to God's promise to Hagar (16:11–12), to God's response to Rebekah's inquiry about her difficulty pregnancy (25:23). Blessings, both human and divine, are often rendered in verse, as in God's blessing of Abraham in 12:3 and Isaac's two blessings in chapter 27 (of Jacob in vv. 27–29 and of Esau in vv. 39–40); but so too are threats and curses, such as Lamech's cryptic threat of violence in 4:23, God's warning after the flood that "whoever sheds the blood of human, / by a human shall that person's blood be shed" (9:6), and Noah's curse of Canaan in 9:25–27. We have seen already the longer, deathbed blessings in the book of Genesis and beyond, and as one moves into other narrative books this trend of using verse to convey authority, gravitas, or solemnity continues, as when God announces the divine name to Moses in Exodus 3:15 ("This is my name forever, / and this my title for all generations"), when Moses remonstrates with the Israelites in the desert when they demand water ("Why do you quarrel with me? / Why do you test the Lord?" [Ex 17:2]), when Joshua commands the sun and moon to stand still ("Sun, stand still at Gibeon, / and Moon, in the valley of Aijalon" [Josh 10:12]), and when Solomon acknowledges the successful founding of the First Temple ("I have built you an exalted house, / a place for you to dwell in forever" [1 Kgs 8:12–13]).

There are two other main ways that poetry functions in biblical narrative, ways that have to do with the specific literary resources of Hebrew verse over against Hebrew prose: the use of figurative language on the one hand, and the expression of interiority on the other. We have identified these as two defining aspects of biblical poetry. In biblical narrative, then, verse functions to introduce both figurative language and the expression of thought and passion into a literary form where it is otherwise mostly absent. This use of verse in biblical narrative seems to be both calculated and subtle, and even though it has been little noted by scholars it is a significant literary technique worth exploring.

Figurative language

One sees the use of figurative language, albeit often fairly simple, throughout for example the snippets of verse attributed to characters in the book of Genesis: "he shall be a wild ass of a man" (16:12); "two nations are in your womb" (25:23); "may God give you of the dew of heaven, / and of the fatness of the earth" (27:28); "you shall break his yoke from your neck" (27:40); "the God who has been my shepherd" (48:15). And one sees it more fully in the long testamentary blessing of Jacob in Genesis 49, where Reuben is called "unstable as water" (v. 3), Judah a "lion's whelp" (v. 9) and one who "washes his garments in wine / and his robe in the blood of grapes; // his eyes are darker than wine, / and his teeth whiter than milk" (vv. 11–12), Issachar a "strong donkey / lying down between sheepfolds" (v. 14), Dan "a snake by the roadside, / a viper along the path, // that bites the horse's heels, / so that the rider falls backwards" (v. 17).

These are just a few examples of the figurative language that fills Jacob's blessing of the tribes of Israel, and can be contrasted with the straightforward literalness with which the blessings are described or enacted in the surrounding prose narrative, as when Jacob describes to Joseph the respective blessings of Manasseh and Ephraim with the prosaic "I know my son, I know; he shall also become a people, and he shall also be great" (48:19), or when he tells Joseph (who is called a "fruitful bough" with branches running over the wall in the poem [49:22]) in very literal terms that "God will be with you and will bring you again to the land of your ancestors" (48:21). And we may notice how terse and nonfigurative is the narrator's comment on Jacob's long blessing: "All these are the twelve tribes of Israel, and this is what their father said to them when he blessed them, blessing each one of them with a suitable blessing" (49:28).

One might also compare in the book of Exodus the straightforward, prosaic description by the narrator of the destruction of the Egyptians at the Red Sea with the pervasive use of metaphor, simile, and mythical language in the poetic Song of the Sea (Ex 15:1–18). The narrator reports: "Moses stretched out his hand over the sea. The LORD drove the sea back by a strong east wind all night, and turned the sea into dry land" (14:21). And while the Israelites walked through on "dry ground," God "clogged the wheels" of the Egyptian chariots, which were caught when "the waters returned and covered the chariots and the chariot drivers," so that finally "Israel saw the Egyptians dead on the seashore" (14:30). Despite the presence of some form of divine intervention, the episode is rendered in a realistic manner, with nary a metaphor to be found.

The poetic rendering of the episode in chapter 15, on the other hand, while not especially elaborate in its figurative language nonetheless makes good use of it. The whole poem is governed by the metaphor "the LORD is a man of war (*ish milhamah,*15:3)," and God's martial acts against the Egyptians are themselves metaphorized, with "fury" imagined as a fire that "consumed them as stubble" (v. 7) and the wind that drove back the sea figured as "the blast of your nostrils" (v. 8). The poem also makes use of a key figure to anchor the three sections of the poem, referring to the image of an inert, weighty object: "they went down into the depths like a stone" (v. 5), "they sank like lead in the mighty waters" (v. 10), and, with reference to the inhabitants of Canaan who look on as the LORD leads the Israelites forward, "they became still as a stone" (v. 16). Although it is never made explicit, it is likely that lying behind the description of the panic manifested by the peoples of Philistia, Edom, Moab, and Canaan in v. 15 is the metaphor of a woman in labor, whose imagined "trembling," "pangs," and "dismay" become a standard trope in biblical poetry for the reaction to military threat (cf. Isa. 13:8 and 21: 3; Ps 48:5–6; Jer 6:24). And while obscured in English translations like the NRSV, the terms for "chiefs" of Edom and "leaders" of Moab (v. 15) are in fact the figurative "bulls" and "rams" in Hebrew. None of this imagery is to be found in the surrounding prose, and its presence here in the Song of the Sea adds vividness, metaphorical complexity, and emotional content to the narrative.

The expression of interiority

This latter aspect, emotional content, points toward the second major contribution of poetry to biblical narrative, namely, its use in the expression or intensification of a character's emotional life, his or her thoughts, feelings, and commitments. We see this in several of the poems we have already looked at, including the Song of the Sea, where the expression of joy and thanksgiving at God's saving action is paramount. We see it too in the Song of Hannah, the first line of which is, after all, "my heart exults in the LORD" (1 Sam. 2:1). The matter-of-fact reporting of Hannah's conceiving of a child in 1 Samuel 1:19–21 ("In due time Hannah conceived and bore a son. She named him Samuel, for she said, 'I have asked him of the LORD'") and the terse report on the passing of his early years in vv. 23–24 ("So the woman remained and nursed her son, until she weaned him. When she had weaned him she took him up…to the house of the LORD at Shiloh, and the child was young") give little indication of the joy that Hannah must have felt at the conception, the birth, and the presence of this long-desired child. By allowing the reader insight into the exultation of

Hannah's heart, the poem also, paradoxically, underscores the unstated pain that surely lies behind the narrator's prosaic note that after bringing young Samuel up to Shiloh "she left him there for the LORD" (1:28).

Perhaps an even more effective example of the meaningful integration of verse into plot and characterization can be found in the book of Ruth. The book is in many ways a classic example of Hebrew narrative, with little access to the inner lives of its characters, despite the fact that their motivations are crucial for how one understands the unfolding of the plot. In two places, however, the narrative shifts into verse form: Ruth's speech in 1:16–17, and Naomi's speech in 1:20–21. I suggest that the author of the book shifts into the poetic mode here precisely in order to give the reader access to the inner lives of Ruth and Naomi, and to signal to the reader that the author is doing so. Although for most of the book we are left to wonder what the characters are thinking, we are given to know, here at the beginning of the story, that Ruth's primary commitment and motivating factor for her actions is her allegiance to Naomi and, further, that Naomi specifically fails to understand that commitment.

As a consequence of this knowledge, the two poetic speeches of chapter 1 set up the two protagonists as the bearers of the fundamental tensions of the plot. One of those tensions is personal: Ruth has expressed a nakedly emotional commitment to Naomi, while Naomi has ignored that commitment and deemed herself "empty" as she returns from Moab. Will Naomi recognize and accept Ruth's commitment to her? A second tension foregrounded by these speeches is theological: Ruth brings up God almost incidentally, as she includes a commitment to "your God" in her larger vow of solidarity with Naomi, but Naomi makes God the center of her speech, referring directly to God four times, and naming God as the primary agent in her life, an agent conceived of, moreover, in an entirely negative light. Will Naomi be confirmed in her dire judgment that God has inflicted calamity upon her and drained her life of meaning and relationship? And whose view of reality is correct here? Is Naomi right to attribute such agency to God, or is Ruth right to focus on human relationships, relegating divine action to the margins?

None of these tensions are finally resolved by the end of the narrative. We are still not sure of how Naomi views either Ruth or God. Recall that it is the women of the neighborhood who declare "blessed be the LORD" upon the birth of Obed [4:14] and who deem Ruth "better to you than seven sons" [4:15]. From Naomi, however, we hear not a word. Naomi does take the child to her bosom we are told (v. 16), and perhaps we are to imagine that she loves and hopes again after the tragedies that have defined her life to this point. Or, perhaps it is obligation or necessity that motivates Naomi to accept Obed into her life. Then, it may well be some combination of these that defines Naomi's inner life at the end of the book, since love and loss are hardly mutually exclusive.

And what of the theological tension between Ruth's and Naomi's view of reality? Here, too much is left up to the reader. The book is in fact much less explicitly theological than is often claimed. Other than God "making Ruth conceive" (4:13; with of course the help of Boaz), all of the action that gets done in the plot gets done by human characters enacting human agency in a world of recognizable human relationships, both personal and social. Indeed, Ruth's solidarity with Naomi is the central driving fact of the narrative, as she first provides food to keep them alive and then provides the heir that Naomi needs to secure her legal rights in Judah. Still, it is certainly possible, as the many theological readings of the story demonstrate, to see God working behind the scenes of the narrative. In the end, this ambiguity too is characteristic of Hebrew narrative, which clearly prefers to hold together human and divine agency, affirming a certain amount of providential guidance in history while also admitting and encouraging human action and moral responsibility.

The book of Ruth, then, makes intentional use of the resources of poetry to add complicating tensions to the plot by providing rare insight into the interiority of its characters, but the opaqueness and ambiguity of the narrative mode remains paramount. Had the poems, with their revelation of inner lives, come near the end of the book, the tensions might be resolved more neatly and we might not be left wondering whether Naomi ever realizes the strength and depth of Ruth's commitment to her, or wondering whether Ruth ever comes to love Boaz, or wondering about the nature of reality and whether God might be said to have an explicit role in the shaping of human destiny. Verse is used strategically to set up the tensions of the plot, but not to solve them.

Poetry and narrative in the book of Job

No treatment of narrative and poetry working together in the Bible would be complete without considering the book of Job. The book of Job is unconventional in several respects, and its combination of narrative and poetry is the reverse of what we see elsewhere in biblical literature. Instead of a predominantly narrative context with inset poems, we have a lengthy book of poetry with very brief narrative sections framing it. Chapters 1 and 2 and most of chapter 42 (vv. 7–27) take the form of prose narrative; the other thirty-nine-plus chapters are in high poetic form, by far the longest sustained poetic work in the Bible. Why, after beginning in the narrative mode, does the book shift into poetry in such a dramatic fashion? Although modern scholarship has tended to answer this question in terms of authorship, positing two or more authors to account for the differences in form, we can also answer it in specifically literary terms, in a way that accounts for the shift from narrative to poetry regardless of the number of authors. That is to say, the book of Job shifts into poetic form because it needs the literary resources of poetry, resources unavailable in prose narrative.

The poetic section of the book of Job is an example of the ancient Near Eastern genre of "literary dialogue," in which a central issue or question is discussed by two or more speakers. None of the other examples of this genre, however, have the sort of narrative frame that we see in the book of Job. And one of the things we may notice is that in Job, the narrative and poetic sections of the book are governed by very different central questions. The poetic section of Job, like its Egyptian and Mesopotamian counterparts, is governed by the question of the nature and origin of suffering, and especially the relationship of suffering to a just deity; or as popularly expressed, "why do bad things happen to good people?" But the opening narrative section of the book (chs. 1 and 2) is governed by a strikingly different question, namely, What is the source of Job's piety? Indeed, "the Adversary" (usually translated as "Satan," but this is not the devil of later Christian thought) announces plainly the question to be explored: "Does Job fear God for naught?" (1:9). The exploration of this question functions as an ironic backdrop to the poetic dialogue, since the question that will occupy Job and his friends for some two dozen chapters is answered for readers right at the very beginning. We as readers know the source of Job's suffering: It is inflicted on him precisely as part of the attempt to solve the defining question of the opening narrative.

What is especially important with regard to literary form is that answering the question posed by the narrative necessitates gaining access to Job's inner life, something that biblical narrative is, as we know, very reluctant to allow. Thus, the central problem driving the plot of the book—namely, the need to access Job's inner life in order to discover the motivation for his piety ("Does Job fear God for naught?")—sets up the move to verse, the preferred form for such access in any sustained way. Beginning in the narrative mode, the book by convention gives precious little insight into Job's thoughts or feelings. But when the story moves to Job's anguished death wish ("Blot out the day of my birth / and the night that announced, 'A man-child is conceived.'"), prose narration gives way to the passionate but finely modulated poetic form of chapter 3, including direct expressions of Job's emotional life ("I feared a fear and it befell me, / and what I dreaded came upon me. // I am not at ease, nor am I quiet; / I have no rest; and trouble arrives" [3:25-26]), followed by many chapters in verse form of Job's impassioned defense of his integrity.

The question of the motivation for Job's piety will be resolved, according to the terms set by the Adversary, by whether or not Job curses God in response to the suffering they agree to inflict on him. If he does, then that will be taken to reveal that his motivation was mercantile in nature, based on the quid pro quo of piety in exchange for a good life. Thus, as Job's inner life spills forth in poetry, readers wait to see whether he will curse or continue to bless God. If he did curse God outright, or by contrast obviously reaffirmed his former simple expressions of faith, the tension of the opening narrative would be quickly resolved and the book brought to a close. To keep that from happening, the author seems to get Job as close as possible to cursing God without actually doing so, as in 3:1-10 when he curses all of God's creation without quite cursing God, so that readers continue to wonder, "Is he cursing God or not?"

Certainly, Job's interlocutors in the book take his words as blasphemous, for it evokes in them an equally impassioned defense of God's justice. As Job's challenges to God escalate throughout the poetry, the friends' attacks on Job escalate as well, to the point that their initial sympathy for him turns to outright condemnation: "Should your babble put others to silence, / and when you mock, shall no one shame you?" (11:3); or "Is not your wickedness great? / There is no end to your iniquities" (22:5). For his part, Job takes time out from his critique of God to call the friends "miserable comforters" speaking "windy words" (16:2-3). Beyond ad hominem attacks, the poetic speeches that dominate the book give both Job and his friends a chance to articulate their competing views of the world, to give expression to, as Carol

Newsom puts it, "a conflict of moral imaginations." Such a sustained expression of thought and passion and articulated worldview, and along with it 90 percent of the book of Job, would be unthinkable in Hebrew prose narrative. The book needs poetry to do what it does.

The book of Job also makes use in spades of figurative language. Metaphor, simile, personification, and a variety of figures of thought pervade the poetry. This aspect of poetic style is not quite so central to the plot of the book in the way that the expression of interiority is, and it is so integrated into the speeches of the characters that it is impossible to summarize easily the many ways figuration functions in the book. But one thing that metaphorical language and imagery does is allow the characters to both express and develop their moral imaginations. They serve, in other words, both rhetorical and intellectual functions. Rhetorically, figurative language gives vividness and "punch" to the worldviews they express. One of Eliphaz's first statements to Job is, "As I have seen, those who plow iniquity / and sow trouble reap the same" (4:8). This is not a particularly creative metaphor ("You reap what you sow"), but it makes concrete what might otherwise be an unimaginative platitude, and it helps to express one of Eliphaz's basic premise, namely, that moral consequences are built into the natural order of things, just as sowing leads to reaping. This is typical of all three of Job's friends, who appeal repeatedly to metaphors from the natural world, precisely because the natural world seems to be a given. If the world, for the friends, is something inarguable, it is also something reliable. It reflects in its regular, discernible patterns the regularity and discernibility of human morality and divine justice. And so Eliphaz imagines the "godless" as barren plants or trees: "They shake off their unripe grape like the vine, / and cast off their blossoms, like the olive tree" (15:33).

Job too will appeal to the natural world for metaphors, though not as often as the friends and to different ends. So, for example, his central theme of the brevity and meaninglessness of human lives

finds expression in several different images from nature. For
example:

> A mortal, born of woman, few of days and full of trouble,
> > comes up like a flower and withers,
> > > flees like a shadow and does not last. (14:1-2)

> But the mountain falls and crumbles away,
> > and the rock is removed from its place;
> the waters wear away the stones;
> > the torrents wash away the soil of the earth;
> > > so you destroy the hope of mortals. (14:18-19)

What is interesting in these lines is the way that Job uses
seemingly antithetical imagery of emphemerality (the flower, the
shadow) and strength (the mountain, the rock) to express the
same point, that human life and achievement, like nature, has
neither meaning nor longevity. Rather than conceding that the
natural world inherently supports the friends moral viewpoint,
he reclaims it in the service of his own.

In addition to the goal of rhetorical persuasion, we see figurative
language giving Job intellectual tools that help him develop
genuinely new ideas. One of the most important and effective
examples of this is his gradual articulation of what is sometimes
called "the forensic metaphor," the idea that the only place that
Job and God could possibly meet on equal terms is in a
courtroom. The figurative nature of this idea (i.e., that it could not
literally happen) is emphasized by Job the first time it occurs to
him: "For he is not a mortal, as I am, that I might answer him, /
that we should come to trial together" (9:32). But the very nature
of metaphor is such that impossible things can be imagined, and if
imagined then also voiced, and such voicings have the power to
open up new lines of thinking and being. And so Job returns to
the forensic metaphor (see especially chs. 13 and 16), finding in it
a way to imagine an equal footing with God that would otherwise

be unavailable ("maintaining the right of a mortal with God" [16:21]). Rather than asserting a de facto divine justice that can be seen inhering in the given world and thus immune to challenge or debate, Job reimagines it as subject to human culture, something to be negotiated and decided in the (metaphorical) courtroom. The theological implications of this position are many and potentially radical, but we note here that they become available only because of the figurative mode of thought and expression that is itself made available by poetic form.

It is not just Job and his friends who make use of a full range of metaphorical language, but God does as well. Finally showing up in Job 38 so to respond to the long debate over human suffering and divine justice that we as readers have just witnessed, God is given by the poet two substantial speeches, in 38:31–39:40 and in 40:6–41:34. The God-speeches are endlessly interpretable, since the poet avoids giving direct answers to the questions of suffering and justice with which the book has been concerned, preferring instead to let God speak line after line of vivid poetry filled with rhetorical questions and with figurative and mythological language. God speaks of morning stars singing with joy at the moment of creation, of the primordial, chaotic sea imagined as an infant in diapers, of "the dwelling place of light," of "the waterskins of heaven," of a warhorse whose neck is "clothed with thunder," and finally of the chaos monsters Behemoth and Leviathan. Leviathan gets the lion's share of attention in the speeches, and some of their most striking similes. "Will you play with it as with a bird, / or will you put it on the leash for your girls?" (41:5), God sarcastically asks Job. Hardly, since "Its sneezes flash forth lightening, / and its eyes are like the eyelids of dawn" (41:18). After being paraded forth by God and admiringly described, Leviathan disappears into the sea, which in his wake "boils like a pot" so that "one would think the deep to be white-haired" (41:31–32).

It is hard to overstate the importance of poetic form for the God-speeches. Rather than giving answers, the poetry gives an experience. Instead of a prose discourse on the nature of theodicy (i.e., the question of divine justice), we get an intense, vibrant vision of the cosmos, a cosmos seemingly unconcerned with humanity and, moreover, filled with the uncontrollable and the incomprehensible. The author could certainly have chosen to write a more straightforward, nonpoetic and nonfigurative "answer" to Job and his friends; but had he or she done so, the only role left to Job and to readers would be to either accept or reject the answer. We experience the poetry in all its complexity, and then we must construct our interpretation of it (either positive or negative), rather than having that interpretation given to us. In other words, we must read it as literature, and as poetry.

Chapter 5
Connections between texts

There is an odd moment near the end of the Oscar-winning film from 1992, *Unforgiven* (directed by Clint Eastwood). In the wake of a chaotic gunfight in a crowded barroom, the character William Munny (played by Eastwood) is about to shoot a wounded Little Bill (played by Gene Hackman), who says unbelievingly, "I don't deserve to die like this...I was building a house." Little Bill is shot and killed just moments later ("It ain't about deserves," says William Munny), but what makes the scene odd is the seeming non sequitur of his reference to building a house. Just how does that relate to whether or not Little Bill deserves to die? As suggested in a fuller treatment by Koosed and Linafelt (1996), it seems likely, given that the film has several other biblical references, that the line alludes to the biblical verse in Deuteronomy 20:5, where the activity of building a house that has not yet been finished and dedicated exempts one from having to go to war. Admittedly, the verse from Deuteronomy is a relatively obscure one, and it is the rare viewer who could be expected to catch the allusion. The movie works fine if the allusion is missed, but catching it adds another layer of meaning, another context for interpretation. And even if one doubts the conscious intentionality of the biblical allusion on the part of the screenwriter, it is still possible to say that the Bible exists as a real if unconscious source text for the film.

Such is the nature of "intertexuality," the name literary scholars have given to the often complex web of relationships that all texts (and other cultural productions) are a part of. No literary work (or film, or song, or speech, or website, etc.) exists in a vacuum but rather grows out of and draws on earlier works. Sometimes the relationship to those earlier works is obvious and intentional, sometimes it is less obvious but still intentional, and sometimes it is neither obvious nor intentional. For some literary scholars the question of intentionality is entirely moot, and intertextuality refers not to conscious, trackable allusions or influences but rather to the vast web of literary, linguistic, and cultural material that forms an essentially infinite depth of background. As Julia Kristeva, one of the prime theorists of intertextuality, puts it, "every text is from the outset under the jurisdiction of other discourses which impose a universe on it." There is certainly value in recognizing the complexities of "a multidimensional space in which a variety of writings, none of them original, blend and clash" (so Roland Barthes), and of admitting that we could never fully comprehend or articulate this web. But by focusing on that more narrow form of intertextuality in the Bible, where we see later authors or texts citing, alluding to, and sometimes parodying earlier authors and texts, we can explore the specific literary connections between texts, connections that contribute to the rich, sometimes conflictual, layers of meaning in biblical literature.

Genesis 1

Let's begin at the beginning, with the very first chapter of the Bible. The story now preserved in Genesis 1:1–2:3 is an ancient Israelite creation story that emerged from official priestly circles in Jerusalem. In it, God creates a livable cosmos out of a preexisting chaos, which is defined by uninterrupted darkness and an endless, watery abyss. (In the biblical account God does not create ex nihilo, or out of nothing, as the later Christian doctrine would have it). Though sometimes flawed in its rendering of the Hebrew syntax and grammar, the King James Bible's version captures well the stately elegance of the original, nowhere more so than in its opening lines: "In the beginning God created the heaven and the earth. And the earth was without form, and void, and darkness was upon the face of the deep" (Gen. 1:1–2). The process of creation begins: "God said, 'Let there be light': and there was light" (v. 3). God declares this new thing, light, to be good, and then divides or separates it from darkness, calling the one Day and the other Night. This process continues over six days, with God alternately speaking new realities into existence and separating them from each other (water, sky, land, plants, animals, and humans), all the while pushing back and constricting the forces of chaos (darkness and the water) until finally creation is complete and God is able to cease from the work of creation on the seventh day, sanctifying that day as the Sabbath, the day of rest.

The story has become justly famous in Western literary and religious culture for its smooth and elegant portrayal of a creator God effortlessly establishing a good and reliable cosmos. And indeed, the story seems to have achieved fame and a certain cultural authority very early in its existence, since despite the fact that it is not the most ancient of biblical creation stories (the garden of Eden story in Gen. 2–3 holds that distinction) it gets cited and alluded to several times by other biblical authors, including the visionary prophet Jeremiah. In chapter 4 of the book of Jeremiah, the prophet gives an imaginative description of the destruction that will come with an invading "foe from the north" (Jer. 4:6), a recurring theme in the book and a reference to the expanding power of Babylon, the empire that would eventually conquer the nation of Judah and sack Jerusalem. Much of chapter 4 contains stereotypical if vivid and moving images of military destruction; but the rhetoric and tone of the chapter shifts in v. 23, as the prophet begins to recount in poetic form a supernatural vision of widespread devastation:

> I beheld the earth, and lo, it was without form and void;
> and the heavens, and they had no light. (Jer. 4:23, KJV)

The poetry signals to the reader a direct engagement with the priestly creation story by way of the key words "earth," "heavens," "light," and most especially the phrase "it was without form and void." In fact, the distinctive latter phrase, in Hebrew a pair of nicely rhyming words, *tohu vabohu*, occurs only here and in Genesis 1. Perhaps best translated as something like "wild and waste" (so Everett Fox) or "welter and waste" (so Robert Alter), the phrase indicates the threatening chaotic state that existed before God's creative activity, an unlivable realm where attempts at existence would be futile. Such futility is represented in Jeremiah's vision by the retreat of living things, as the "birds of the air" disappear and human life vanishes from a once fruitful and productive earth (v. 25). The two things that God counterposed in Genesis 1 to the chaos of darkness and the watery abyss have here disappeared (the light in v. 23) or become fundamentally unstable (the earth in v. 24). It is a vision of destruction that takes the form of a complete dismantling or reversal of the original act of creation, and its rhetorical force depends on the reader knowing the precursor story in some detail.

But what is the force of this vision? Why does the prophet make such explicit use of the priestly creation story? There can be no single correct answer to these questions, but readers are meant to ask them and to ponder them, and I can imagine a couple of ways that one might pursue interpretation. One is to notice the intentionality with which the political is fused with the cosmic. The prophet uses imagery of resurgent cosmic disorder to express the realities of political and social disorder that come with extended warfare, siege, and eventually the destruction of a city and a political state. For those living through such dire times it feels like "the end of the world." Secondly, the prophet brings to bear on this political and social chaos a theological perspective: It was God who first brought order and existence out of the disorder and futility of original chaos, and it is God who now is responsible for the reversion we see envisioned. On the one hand this makes the destruction inevitable and therefore the prospects for Judah all the more bleak:

> For this shall the earth mourn,
>> and the heavens above be black:
> because I have spoken it, I have purposed it,
>> and will not repent, neither will I turn back from it. (Jer. 4:28, KJV)

On the other hand, it also means that there is some small hope for a future beyond the destruction, since God has the capacity to begin creation all over again. This latter hope is expressed briefly in the last phrase of v. 27:

> For this hath the LORD said,
> "The whole land shall be desolate;
>> yet I will not make a full end." (Jer. 4:27, KJV)

If Jeremiah 4 reverses Genesis 1 in order to evoke political disorder and to identify God as the agent behind that disorder, we see in chapter 3 of the book of Job a very different use of the chaos/creation theme, one in which the experience of chaos evoked is personal rather than political and in which the agent of reversion is human rather than divine. Job begins the passage by cursing the day of his birth, but quickly extends that to a curse of all creation in terms that pointedly reverse the creative acts of God in Genesis 1. For example, in place of God's "Let there be light" (Gen. 1:3), there is Job's "let there be darkness" (Job 3:4). And by calling on God's ancient enemy Leviathan in 3:8, "Let those curse it [darkness, night] who curse the Sea, those who are skilled to rouse up Leviathan," Job aligns himself with the forces of chaos rather than that of order. Or perhaps it is better said that Job experiences the suffering and destruction that have overtaken him as radically chaotic, and thus he sees the chaos monster Leviathan as a natural ally.

It is very likely that that author of Job 3 knew not only Genesis 1 but also the passage from Jeremiah 4, and that we find then an intertextual relationship to the second power, so to speak. In fact, the Job poet seems to combine two passages from Jeremiah, the anticreation vision of Jeremiah 4 with Jeremiah's own curse of his birth found in chapter 20:14. In Jeremiah the two passages represent entirely distinct genres and have no overlap, but the Job poet brings them together, projecting Job's individual experience of chaos onto the world at large and perceiving in the tragic ruin of a single life a larger problem within the order of the creation. For Job, unlike Jeremiah, the personal is the cosmological. By considering the reuse of Genesis 1 in both Jeremiah 4 and Job 3, combined there with Jeremiah 20, we see intentionally nuanced variations in specific themes from earlier texts, such nuance being a hallmark of the literary imagination.

The iconoclasm of the Job poet

Of all biblical authors, the Job poet is perhaps the most intentional about repurposing earlier texts, often doing so with a dollop of irony and even parody. Though there was of course no "Bible" per se for the author of Job, he seems to relish alluding to, and generally subverting, texts and ideas with a certain cultural authority, as we saw earlier with the priestly creation story. We see it also in Job, chapter 7, where the poet engages in a bitter parody of Psalm 8, v. 4. Psalm 8 is a classic example of an ancient Hebrew "hymn of praise," locating the goodness and reliability of God in the wonders of the created world, declaring in its opening and closing lines, "how majestic is your name in all the earth." If the poem is thus framed by a confession of God's majesty, it is nevertheless the case that a celebration of humanity is both literally and figuratively at the center of the poem. The speaker in Psalm 8 claims that humans have been made just "a little lower than God" (a common alternative rendering of the line is "a little lower than the angels") and have been "crowned with glory and honor" (v. 5), with God giving them "dominion over the works of

[God's] hands" (v. 6). And right at the very center of the poem, in a perfectly balance poetic couplet, the speaker wonders,

> What are human beings that you are mindful of them,
>> mortals that you care for them? (v. 4)

And so a hymn of praise for God's good creation becomes a poem celebrating humanity's role as the crown of that creation, a role made possible only by God's mindful attention to an otherwise undeserving human creature.

Now, let us see what the iconoclastic Job poet does with this iconic hymn of praise. The author signals to the reader an engagement with Psalm 8 by directly quoting the first phrase of that central couplet on the nature of humanity: "What are human beings...?" (Job 7:17). And for just a moment, as the question unfolds, it seems that the Job poet is on the same triumphant page as the psalmist:

> What are human beings, that you make so much of them,
>> that you set your mind on them?

The phrase rendered by the NRSV as "that you make so much of them" more literally means "that you make them great." In other words, it seems as if the poet is here recognizing and celebrating the "greatness" of humanity as asserted by Psalm 8.

The tone begins to change, however, as the poet has Job ask in 7:18 why it is that God "visits them every morning" and then "tests them every moment." The idea of God "visiting" humanity is potentially positive, and indeed it is the same Hebrew word used in Psalm 8 to mean "care," but by the time we get to the idea of God constantly "testing" humanity, the tone of bitterness begins to emerge only to come fully to the surface in v. 19:

> Will you not look away from me for a while,
>> let me alone until I swallow my spittle?

And so we realize the sarcasm with which the Job poet imbues his or her quoting of the earlier psalmic language. The question of why God "cares *for*" humanity enough to elevate them above the rest of creation undeservedly becomes a question of why God "cares *about*" humanity so much that God cannot stop scrutinizing and testing them, again undeservedly. The grateful acknowledgment in Psalm 8 of God's unwarranted attention to humans becomes in the mouth of Job a bitter rejection of God's unwarranted attention. In contrast to the lofty and noble, even transcendent, portrayal of humanity in that psalm of praise, Job's protest focuses in on the smallest and most physically mundane of actions: all he asks is for a moment to "swallow his spit."

On the one hand, the sarcastic citation of Psalm 8 here functions to express Job's personal sense of extreme exposure and cosmic claustrophobia: What could he possibly have done to deserve such intense and negative scrutiny from God? On the other hand, the intertextual relationship set up with the psalm goes beyond just Job's personal experience, challenging the larger conception of humanity and its relationship to the created world. For while Psalm 8 wants to imagine humankind ruling creation as God's vice-regent ("You have given them dominion over the works of your hands," v. 6), Job prefers to imagine humans as slave-laborers, bound to a life of "hard service on earth" (7:1–2). For Job, humans not only do not rule over creation, they do not even rule over their own lives, which is one of the implications of the slave metaphor. Rather than meaningful lives of active agency, humans are allotted "months of emptiness" and "nights of misery" (7:30). Their hard labor gains them nothing, and they are ruled over by an all-seeing and far-from-benevolent taskmaster. Instead of expecting "glory and honor" from God, Job asks only for a single moment of freedom, just long enough to swallow.

There are several other examples in Job of these sorts of iconoclastic references to earlier, more traditionally acceptable texts, as for example when Job pleads, "O earth, do not cover my blood" (16:18). In the Bible's primal story of murder, found in Genesis 4, Cain kills his brother Abel, whose blood cries out from the earth for justice. By placing an allusion to this story in the mouth of Job, who throughout the chapter imagines God violently assaulting him ("he slashes open my kidneys...he rushes at me like a warrior" [16:13–14]), the author boldly imagines God in the place of Cain the archetypal murderer. But let us close this section on Job by looking at what is perhaps the final intertextual allusion in the book, found near the very end in the short prose narrative conclusion in chapter 42.

After all that Job has suffered, and following God's extended speech in chapters 38–41, we are told that "the LORD restored the fortunes of Job...and the LORD gave Job twice as much as he had before" (42:10). At first blush, this would seem to be a straightforward description of Job's newly restored prosperity. Part of the testing of Job at the beginning of the book entailed taking away "all that he has" (1:10, 11, 12) to see what his response would be; and now that the testing is over, Job's material wealth is returned. But we notice that he is given back by God "twice as much" as he had before, and we may be given to wonder if there is some significance in the twofold restoration of Job's wealth—Why not just restore everything as before? Why *twice* as much? The answer to this question may well lie in a very subtle intertextual connection between the book of Job and the book of Exodus. In the section of Exodus (chs. 20–23) known by scholars as "the Covenant Code," which presents a variety of legal and ethical precepts, we find that one of the stipulated consequences for a thief caught stealing is to "pay back double" (22:4, 7, and 9) what was taken. Is it possible that God is being compared here to a thief? A thief who was caught stealing Job's life, and who now has to "pay back double" all that he stole? Now, it is not entirely clear that this is an intentional allusion, to be sure. But in a book that makes so many intertextual allusions, it certainly is a strong possibility. Some readers often assume that no biblical author would entertain strongly negative ideas about God, but we've already seen the Job author compare God to Cain the murderer; after that, the metaphor of God-as-thief seems positively mild.

If one does take this allusion to the caught thief of Exodus 22 as being intentional, it becomes potentially very important for interpreting the book as a whole. Readers arriving at the end of the book of Job are often strongly divided between those who feel that God is portrayed as being in the right and those who think God has behaved very badly toward Job. But anyone who accepts Job 42:10 as an allusion to the legal code from Exodus will have a hard time defending a wholly positive portrait of God. The implied metaphor of God-as-thief necessarily puts God in the wrong, even as it seems to justify Job's claim to having been mistreated by God. This in turn may affect one's evaluation of other passages in the book, as for example Job's final response to God in 42:2–6 and God's long speeches to Job in chapters 38 through 41. Job's response to God can be interpreted either very negatively or very positively, and if one accepts that the book portrays God as a thief, then the negative reading becomes more plausible. Likewise, God's speeches to Job have been seen as both a wholly satisfying revelation, on the one hand, and a bullying assertion of divine power on the other. Again, accepting an allusion to Exodus 22 in the epilogue to the book might push readers more toward the latter reading of the divine speeches. Of course, one might say that an opposite dynamic is at play in one's interpretation of the ending of Job; that is, that depending on how one feels about the justice of God to that point in the book, one is more or less likely, as the case may be, to accept Job 42:10 as an allusion to Exodus 22. As usual, the biblical narrator does not tell us what to think, and the allusion if intentional is a very subtle one, so the process of interpretation is by necessity an active and inexact task.

Expanding beyond Genesis 1 and Job

One might conclude, based on the examples treated so far in this chapter, that the sort of intertextual relationships we have seen are limited to especially influential texts like the Priestly creation story or to particular authors like the author of the book of Job. But in fact, the practice of quoting, alluding to, or echoing earlier texts is widespread in the Hebrew Bible; it reaches across authors, time periods, and genres as, for example, with the short, often unnoticed book of Lamentations.

The book of Lamentations is a series of five poems of lament over the fall of Jerusalem, Judah's capital city, which was destroyed by the Babylonian army in 587 BCE, with much of the population either killed or taken into exile. Several different speaking voices are present in the poems, including a sort of witness who surveys the damage in parts of chapters 1, 2, and 4 ("How lonely sits the city, / that once was full of people" [1:1]), a representative suffering man who speaks throughout most of chapter 3 ("I am the man who has seen affliction / under the rod of God's wrath" [3:1]), and a first-person communal voice that shows up briefly in chapters 3 (vv. 40–47) and 4 (vv. 17–22) and more fully in chapter 5 ("Our inheritance has been turned over to strangers, / our homes to aliens" [5:2]). But perhaps the most powerfully affecting voice in the book is that of personified Jerusalem, where the conquered city itself is represented as a woman, "Zion" or "daughter Zion," with the former inhabitants of the city represented as her dead or missing children. The "witness" voice begins the book by imagining Zion sitting alone, "weeping bitterly in the night" with "no one to comfort her" (1:2), though the speaker's tone is dispassionate and descriptive rather than emotionally engaged. But in v. 9 of the first chapter, Zion interrupts the speaker to address God with a brief, demanding imperative, "Look, O LORD, at my suffering, / how the enemy triumphs." Though only two lines in length, the interruption seems to sway the original speaker, recruiting him to Zion's cause, as he too then addresses God for the first time in the second-person (1:10). Zion then interrupts again in 1:12, "Look, O LORD, and pay attention, / how abject I have become," and after this point speaks more fully, emphasizing especially the plight of her children: "for these things I weep... my children are ravaged, / for the enemy has triumphed" (1:16); "Listen all you peoples, / notice my pain. // My girls and my boys / have gone into captivity" (1:18; cf. 2:21).

As the book goes on, the originally dispassionate voice of the witness, who may in fact represent the poet as many interpreters think, appropriates the emotional language used by Zion: "My eyes are spent with weeping; my stomach churns" (2:11). The once objective-sounding onlooker becomes more and more an advocate for Zion, encouraging her in her demand for divine justice for herself and her children ("Pour out your heart like water, / before the presence of the LORD. // Lift your hands to him, / for the lives of your children" [2:19]). Zion responds in just this way in 2:20–22, ending her speech with a dual focus on the wrath of God and the fate of her metaphorical children:

> On the day of the LORD's wrath,
>   None survived or escaped.
> Those I have borne and nurtured,
>   my enemy has ruthlessly destroyed.

This is the last we hear from Zion in terms of direct speech. Her appeal to God goes unanswered in the book, though the communal voice in chapter 4 will refer to both Zion and her "precious children" (4:2) in the third person and will lament the "blazing anger" of God that led to the destruction of Jerusalem/Zion.

Although God is referred and addressed and implored, God never appears in the book as a speaker and never responds to the appeals and accusations. The book ends with this plaintive appeal:

> Why have you utterly forgotten us,
>   forsaken us for so long?
> Bring us back to you, O LORD, that we may be restored;
>   renew our days as of old.

> For if you have truly rejected us,
>> and are angry with us beyond measure...
>>> (Lam. 5:20-21, author's trans.)

I have provided here my own translation of the lines from the Hebrew to demonstrate the open-ended quality of the book's conclusion. The final two lines take the form of an incomplete conditional statement, an "if" without a "then": an appropriate end to a book that has relentlessly focused on the devastated city and its inhabitants, and has steadfastly refused to represent the voice of a now-absent God. The book stands as a witness to the ruins of history, refusing to move beyond lament to praise or to some statement of confidence, a move that characterizes nearly every lament in the book of Psalms. The book of Lamentations is simply left opening out into the freighted emptiness of God's silence.

Until, that is, some three or four decades later, when the anonymous prophet (often called Second Isaiah) decides to provide God's missing response. The name "Second Isaiah" can be used to refer either to chapters 40—55 of the book of Isaiah or to the anonymous figure behind these chapters. Although more complicated reconstructions of the history of the authorship and editing of Isaiah have arisen in recent decades, modern scholarship has tended to divide this long prophetic book into three distinct sections. First Isaiah refers to chapters 1–39, much of which is attributed to or at least associated with the eighth-century BCE prophet Isaiah ben Amoz, also known as Isaiah of Jerusalem; Second Isaiah refers to chapters 40–55 and is attributed to an unnamed prophet living in the mid-sixth-century BCE; and Third Isaiah refers to chapters 56–66, usually dated to sometime later in the sixth century, although sometimes more closely associated with or attributed to the same figure behind Second Isaiah.

Whatever the editorial history of the book of Isaiah as we now have it, it is clear that the poetry of chapters 40–55 is one of the great literary achievements of ancient Israel. Poem structure, lineation, and metaphor are handled with great skill by the poet/prophet, and the theological content is sometimes startlingly original and effective. Writing late in the exilic period—those five decades or so after the Babylonian conquest of Judah, when a community of survivors was living in Babylon—the poetry envisions an end to the exile, a resettlement of the land of Judah, and a rebuilding of Jerusalem. It does so, however, not in the form of a political or theological tract but through the highly imaginative and rhetorically charged resources of poetry. Rather than just describing or asserting the new reality to come, the literature poetically imagines both the crumbling power of the once-invincible Babylon and the newly restored status of powerless Judah. The task of the prophet is summed up in the first lines of Second Isaiah, when God announces: "Comfort, O comfort my people, says your God. Speak tenderly to Jerusalem" (Isa. 40:1).

And speak tenderly to Jerusalem the prophet does. The author of Second Isaiah has read the book of Lamentations, and seems to want to respond directly to it, indeed to take on the role of the witness/poet from Lamentations but to now provide the response from God that the original poet was unable or unwilling to imagine. The poet in Lamentations exhorted Zion to cry out to the LORD, to pour out her heart, and to lift up her hands to God on behalf of her children. Now Second Isaiah writes:

> Get you up to a high mountain,
>> O Zion, herald of good tidings;
> lift up your voice with strength,
>> O Jerusalem, herald of good tidings,
>> lift it up, do not fear;
> say to the cities of Judah,
>> "Here is your God!" (40:9)

The language of strong appeal is brought over from Lamentations, but now with the decisive missing piece: "Here is your God." And

Isaiah 40–55 goes on to provide an extended response to the appeals voiced in Lamentations.

One especially interesting example of this intertextual responsiveness to Lamentations can be found in Isaiah 49. Picking up on that final, desperate appeal at the end of Lamentations, "Why have you utterly forgotten us, / forsaken us for so long?" (Lam. 5:20), Second Isaiah puts the following response into the mouth of God: "But Zion said, 'The LORD has forsaken me, / my LORD has forgotten me'" (Isa. 49:14). Second Isaiah takes over the crucial word-pair, "forsaken" and "forgotten," in a common chiastic or reverse order, but which transforms the word-pair into an affirmation that God does *not* forget and does *not* forsake. The recollection of this word-pair is not easily explained as a coincidence. Although the words are, separately, relatively common in the Bible, they occur together only rarely and never elsewhere with God as the subject who "forgets" and "forsakes." While there seems little doubt that the reference here is to Lamentations 5:20, it is true that Zion is not in fact the *speaker* in Lamentations 5:20, which occurs in the context of a communal lament. But in the exilic milieu of Second Isaiah, the personified city Zion dominates the horizon of the nation Judah. All Judahite speech for Second Isaiah has been subsumed under the figure of Zion, the city/woman lamenting the loss of her inhabitants/ children.

In order to answer Zion's complaint, the poet in a daring metaphorical turn has God assume the persona of a mother:

Can a woman forget her nursing child,
or show no compassion for the child of her womb?
Even if these could forget,
yet I will not forget you. (Isa. 49:15)

The poet chooses here the one metaphor that can begin perhaps to answer the rhetoric of Lamentations: God as a mother who also laments and hopes for the return of her children. As some commentators point out, the metaphor might well be rooted in the biological necessity of the new mother to nurse: even if she could forget her child, her body will remind her. This is not the first time that the poet of Second Isaiah has used physical metaphors of birthing or mothering to imagine God. In chapter 42, God is compared both to a warrior and to a woman in labor:

> The LORD goes forth like a soldier,
>   like a warrior he stirs up his fury;
> he cries out, he shouts aloud,
>   he shows himself mighty against his foes.
> "For a long time I have held my peace,
>   I have kept still and restrained myself;
> now I will cry out like a woman in labor,
>   I will gasp and pant. (Isa. 42:13–14)

We see here the startling creativity of the poet, bringing together two images that seem to be conceptually very far apart. Both warrior and woman-in-labor are used as synonymous metaphors for the violent agitation that God will display in the act of freeing God's people and returning them to their land. But of course the labor image adds something missing in the warrior image, namely an irrepressible biological basis for the actions of God. A warrior must "stir up" his fury to cry aloud, but a woman in labor is gripped by forces outside her control and cannot stop the crying aloud that is sure to come. By using the feminine imagery of birth and nursing-motherhood in chapters 42 and 49, the poet has imagined an undeniable biological basis for God's saving action on behalf of exiled Judah, and he has done so in such a way as to both invoke and transcend feminine stereotypes. While a nursing mother thinking of her child is conventional (until applied to God!), the idea of a woman's labor pangs representing the furious strength of a warrior is very unconventional indeed.

As it happens the unconventionality of the latter image, and our poet's intense creativity, is underscored by just the sort of intertextual relationship with which the present chapter is concerned. The poet of Second Isaiah does not invent the poetic image of a woman in labor, which seems rather to have been a common motif in prophetic poetry. Twice the earlier Isaiah of Jerusalem uses the image. The first time describes the response of the Babylonians to the coming divine judgment:

> Therefore all hands will be feeble,
> and every human heart will melt,
> and they will be dismayed.
> Pangs and agony will seize them;
> anguish like a woman in labor.
> They will look aghast at one another;
> their faces will be aflame. (Isa. 13:7–8)

The second instance in First Isaiah describes the prophet's own response to the experience of being seized by divine ecstasy and the resulting "stern vision" that he receives:

> Therefore my loins are filled with anguish;
> pangs have seized me,
> like the pangs of a woman in labor;
> I am bowed down so that I cannot hear,
> I am dismayed so that I cannot see. (Isa. 21:3)

And the prophet Jeremiah, imagining a stereotypical invading "enemy from the north" coming against the city of Zion, describes the population's response this way:

> "We have heard news of them,
> our hands fall helpless;
> anguish has taken hold of us,
> pain as of a woman in labor." (Jer. 6:24)

There are other examples of this motif, but these three make clear the common usage of the metaphor of woman in labor: it seems to have always been used to represent fear, panic, and helplessness in the face of some threat, and it is always applied to humans. Until, of course, Second Isaiah comes along and reappropriates this metaphor, applying it to God. In doing so, our prophet transforms the metaphor from one that evokes human dread and weakness to one that evokes divine power and efficacy. Further, this transformation is made without changing the bodily based manifestations of labor that lie at the heart of the image. Both the conventional use of the image and the startling reuse of it by Second Isaiah draw on the same physical experience that inevitably comes with childbirth, but in using that physicality to imagine God intervening on behalf of oppressed Israel, Second Isaiah has converted the traditionally negative prophetic image of a woman-in-labor into an unexpectedly positive theological metaphor.

More connections

The examples treated above represent a small selection indeed of the many fruitful connections between texts that can found in the Bible. As a next step, one might examine the links between Hagar's story in Genesis 16 and the Exodus story; the book of Esther and the books of Samuel; Ruth's nighttime scene with a tipsy Boaz and Lot's drunken seduction by his daughters in Genesis 19; the story of Joseph in Genesis 39 with that of Tamar in 2 Samuel 13; or Amos's prophetic critique of economic injustice and the ethical codes of the Torah, to name just a few more. Naturally, not every reader can be expected to know the content of the Bible well enough to notice all or even most of the connections. The more one reads, the more one is likely to be aware of the allusions and influences in any given passage; but having an annotated Bible at hand will help as well. Not every passage in the Bible contains the sort of connections we have seen, but a surprising number do and catching them almost always makes for a fuller and more interesting reading.

References

Introduction

Longinus, *On the Sublime.* trans. D. A. Russell, in *Ancient Literary Criticism* (Oxford: Oxford University Press, 1972).

Augustine, *Confessions*, trans. Henry Chadwick (Oxford: Oxford University Press, 1991).

Vladimir Nabokov, *Lectures on Literature* (New York: Harcourt, Brace, Jovanovich, 1980).

Mary Karr, introduction to *The Wasteland and Other Writings*, by T. S. Eliot (New York: Random House, 2001).

Chapter 1: Biblical literature and the Western literary tradition

Homer, *The Iliad*, trans. Robert Fagles (New York: Penguin Books, 1990).

Erich Auerbach, "Odysseus' Scar," in *Mimesis*, trans. Willard R. Trask (Princeton, NJ: Princeton University Press, 1953).

Robert Lowth, *De Sacra Poesi Hebraeorum Praelectiones Academicae Oxonii Habitae* (London: Clarendon, 1753). English translation of the 4th edition published as *Lectures on the Sacred Poetry of the Hebrews*, trans. G. Gregory (London: Thomas Tegg, 1839).

Terry Eagleton, *How to Read a Poem* (Oxford: Blackwell, 2007).

T. S. Eliot, preface to the 2nd edition of *The Sacred Wood: Essays on Poetry and Criticism* (London: Methuen, 1928).

Chapter 2: Reading biblical narrative

Jane Smiley, *13 Ways of Looking at the Novel* (New York: Alfred A. Knopf, 2005).

James Wood, *How Fiction Works* (New York: Farrar, Straus and Giroux, 2008).

Erich Auerbach, "Odysseus' Scar," in *Mimesis*, trans. Willard R. Trask (Princeton, NJ: Princeton University Press, 1953).

Chapter 3: Reading biblical poetry

Robert Frost, "Conversations on the Craft of Poetry," in *Collected Prose, Poems, and Plays* (New York: Library of America, 1995).

Marcia Falk, *The Song of Songs: A New Translation and Interpretation* (New York: Harper Collins, 1990).

Robert Lowth, *De Sacra Poesi Hebraeorum Praelectiones Academicae Oxonii Habitae* (London: Clarendon, 1753). English translation of the 4th edition published as *Lectures on the Sacred Poetry of the Hebrews*, trans. G. Gregory (London: Thomas Tegg, 1839).

F. I. Andersen and A. D. Forbes, "'Prose Particle' Counts of the Hebrew Bible," in *The Word of the Lord Shall Go Forth*, ed. C. L. Meyers and M. O'Connor (Winona Lake, WI: Eisenbrauns, 1983).

David Noel Freedman, "Poetry, Pottery, and Prophecy: An Essay on Biblical Poetry," *Journal of Biblical Literature* 96:1 (1977).

Robert S. Kawashima, *Biblical Narrative and the Death of the Rhapsode* (Bloomington: Indiana University Press, 2004).

Terry Eagleton, *How to Read a Poem* (Oxford: Blackwell, 2007).

Robert Alter, *Genesis: Translation and Commentary* (New York: W. W. Norton, 1996).

J. A. Cuddon, *A Dictionary of Literary Terms and Literary Theory*, 3rd ed. (Oxford: Blackwell, 1977).

Chapter 4: Narrative and poetry working together

Shemaryahu Talmon, "Did There Exist a Biblical National Epic?" in *Proceedings of the Seventh World Congress of Jewish Studies, Studies in the Bible and the Ancient Near East* (Jerusalem: World Union of Jewish Studies, 1981).

Carol Newsom, *The Book of Job: A Contest of Moral Imaginations* (New York: Oxford University Press, 2003).

Chapter 5: Connections between texts

Jennifer Koosed and Tod Linafelt, "How the West Was Not One: Delilah Deconstructs the Western," in *Biblical Glamour and Hollywood Glitz, Semeia* 74 (Atlanta: Scholars Press, 1996).

Julia Kristeva, *La Révolution du Langage Poétique* (Paris: Seuil, 1974);
quoted in Jonathan Culler, *The Pursuit of Signs: Semiotics,
Literature, Deconstruction* (London: Routledge, 1981).

Roland Barthes, *Image–Music–Text*, trans. Stephen Heath (London:
Fontana Press, 1977).

Everett Fox, *The Five Books of Moses: A New Translation with
Introductions, Commentary, and Notes* (New York: Schocken,
1995).

Robert Alter, *Genesis: Translation and Commentary* (New York:
W. W. Norton, 1996).

Gerard Manley Hopkins, "God's Grandeur," in *The Major Works*
(Oxford World's Classics; New York: Oxford University Press,
2002).

Further reading

Alter, Robert. *The Art of Biblical Narrative*. Rev. ed. New York: Basic Books, 2011.

Alter, Robert. *The Art of Biblical Poetry*. Rev. ed. New York: Basic Books, 2011.

Auerbach, Erich. "Odysseus' Scar." In *Mimesis: The Representation of Reality in Western Literature*, translated by Willard R. Trask. Princeton, NJ: Princeton University Press, 1953.

Beal, Timothy K., and David M. Gunn, *Reading Bibles, Writing Bodies: Identity and the Book*. London: Routledge, 1997.

Berlin, Adele. *The Dynamics of Biblical Parallelism*. Bloomington: Indiana University Press, 1985.

Berlin, Adele. *Poetics and Interpretation of Biblical Narrative*. Sheffield, UK: The Almond Press, 1983.

Bible and Culture Collective. *The Postmodern Bible*. New Haven, CT: Yale University Press, 1995.

Brueggemann, Walter, and Tod Linafelt. *An Introduction to the Old Testament: Canon and Christian Imagination*. Louisville, KY: Westminster John Knox Press, 2012.

Dobbs-Allsopp, F. W. *On Biblical Poetry*. New York: Oxford University Press, 2015.

Fewell, Danna Nolan. *Reading between Texts: Intertextuality and the Hebrew Bible*. Louisville, KY: Westminster John Knox Press, 1992.

Fisch, Harold. *Poetry with a Purpose: Biblical Poetics and Interpretation*. Bloomington: Indiana University Press, 1988.

Fokkelman, J. P. *Reading Biblical Narrative: An Introductory Guide*. Translated by Ineke Smit. Louisville, KY: Westminster John Knox Press, 1999.

Fokkelman, J. P. *Reading Biblical Poetry: An Introductory Guide.* Translated by Ineke Smit. Louisville, KY: Westminster John Knox Press, 2001.

Gunn, David M., and Danna Nolan Fewell. *Narrative in the Hebrew Bible.* New York: Oxford University Press, 1993.

Kawashima, Robert. *Biblical Narrative and the Death of the Rhapsode.* Bloomington: Indiana University Press, 2004.

Kugel, James L. *The Idea of Biblical Poetry: Parallelism and Its History.* Baltimore: Johns Hopkins University Press, 1981.

Linafelt, Tod. "On Biblical Style." *St. John's Review* 54 (2012): 17–42.

Miles, Jack. *God: A Biography.* New York: Alfred A. Knopf, 1995.

Norton, David. *A History of the English Bible as Literature.* Cambridge: Cambridge University Press, 2000.

Sherwood, Yvonne. *Biblical Blaspheming: Trials of the Sacred for a Secular Age.* Cambridge: Cambridge University Press, 2014.

Sternberg, Meir. *The Poetics of Biblical Narrative: Ideological Literature and the Drama of Reading.* Bloomington: Indiana University Press, 1987.

Index

Index